MINI

CYPRUS

YOUR TAILOR-MADE TRIP
STARTS HERE

Tailor-made trips and unique adventures crafted by local experts

HOW ROUGHGUIDES.COM/TRIPS WORKS

STEP 1

Pick your dream destination, tell us what you want and submit an enquiry.

STEP 2

Fill in a short form to tell your local expert about you[r] dream trip and preferences

STEP 3

Our local expert will craft your tailor-made itinerary. You'll be able to tweak and refine it until you're completely satisfied.

STEP 4

Book online with ease, pac[k] your bags and enjoy the trip! Our local expert will be on hand 24/7 while you're on the road.

PLAN AND BOOK YOUR TRIP AT
ROUGHGUIDES.COM/TRIPS

How to download your Free eBook

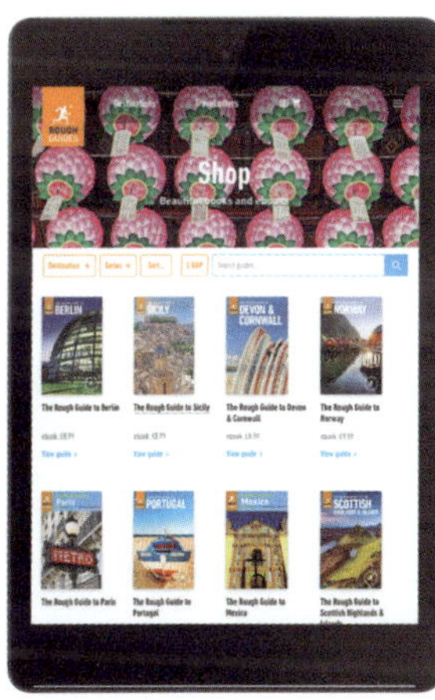

1. Visit **www.roughguides.com/free-ebook** or scan the **QR code** opposite

2. Enter the code **cyprus549**

3. Follow the simple step-by-step instructions

For troubleshooting contact: mail@roughguides.com

Contents

Introduction

Cyprus rose to prominence in antiquity from its copper deposits – indeed the island's name is the basis for the Latin word for the metal (cuprum). In modern times, Cyprus' greatest natural resource is sunshine, over 300 days of it per year. Yet 'Aphrodite's Island' has often been careless with the coastline that puts all that sunshine to good use. Many resorts are large and over-developed, and the battle to preserve the remaining unspoiled coastline is being closely fought. Delve inland for a greater appreciation of this island: countless ancient sites, sleepy villages, frescoed country churches, terraced hillside vineyards and rugged mountain ranges await you. The layers of a long and tangled history, from Stone Age peoples, through Greeks, Phoenicians, Persians, Romans, Byzantines, Crusaders,

WHEN TO GO

From **April** to **October**, you can blissfully enjoy Cyprus' sunshine and sandy shores. Outdoor activities and festivals thrive during this period, and you'll have no trouble getting flights, hotels and tours – although possibly at inflated prices. If you visit between July and August, beware of the fierce heat and overcrowded beaches.

The **autumn**, too, can be remarkably hot and humid, up until September or even October, but you can still enjoy local festivals then. The best time to visit Cyprus is **spring**, when skies are blue, the air is warm and balmy, the uplands are a luxuriant green, and there are wildflowers everywhere.

Much of this advice applies to the **north** as well. Its coast can be cooler than the rest of the island thanks to mountain breezes from the Kyrenia Range.

During **winter** your experience of Cypriot life is likely to be far more authentic and less touristy. As the Ministry of Tourism aims to make Cyprus a year-round destination, you can explore a winter wonderland and free, crafty workshops at the Christmas Villages, and even ski in the Troodos Mountains.

Venetians, Genoese, Ottomans and British, are there to be seen and felt.

Cypriots are a friendly, generous people

Some of your finest memories are likely to be of a remarkably friendly and hospitable people – both Greek-Cypriot and Turkish-Cypriot – despite their turbulent and traumatic recent history. This is, after all, an island that was invaded by Turkey and split in two in 1974. Within weeks, some 180,000 Greek Cypriots were forced to flee to the south of the island, becoming refugees in their own country. Within a year, around 44,000 Turkish Cypriots had moved north. The island is still divided today, though since 2003 there has been greater freedom of movement across the de facto border.

Although it's simple to visit the North (which only Turkey recognizes as a separate republic), most travellers still choose the Greek-Cypriot South. But for those who do cross the cease-fire line that separates the two parts of the island, the North offers the best Lusignan and Venetian monuments, some excellent beaches and appealingly empty landscapes.

An easy-going people

Through all the turmoil, the Cypriots have managed to retain a sunny, relaxed disposition. Ask a couple harvesting grapes if you can take their photo, and they will likely not only strike a happy

The UNESCO-listed church of Archangelos Michail in Pedoulas

pose, but also gather a large bag of grapes for you to take home. Compliment a chef on the quality of his *sheftaliá* at a family-run taverna and he's bound to sit at your table for a chat. It is rare that a visitor leaves Cyprus without some tale of the people's generosity.

It is not a mere marketing gimmick that often at the end of a meal, coffee and a liqueur (either citrus-flavoured or the clear spirit *zivania*) is provided on the house. You don't have to go to the most remote mountain village for such hospitality, but it is also true that you are much less likely to find this warmth in the more obviously tourist-oriented watering holes.

Troubled relations

A more sombre note is struck when the matter of the divided island is raised. Greek-Cypriot refugees from the North react more with melancholy than anger. Nostalgically, restaurants in Larnaka may bear the names of their lost homes in Famagusta. Turkish-Cypriot refugees from the South can be equally as nostalgic with a troubled identity about where they belong. Though now, by preference they can work, and seek education and healthcare in the South. With the opening of the checkpoints and permits to live and work in the South, Greek and Turkish Cypriots have come into closer contact with one another, taking the edge off some resentments, but others linger.

Cyprus has been beset by unwelcome visitors throughout its history. Apart from attracting conquerors from Phoenicia, Egypt, Persia, Greece and Anatolia, Cyprus was easy prey for Latin crusaders and the Venetian republic, and was a pawn in the last days of the British Empire.

The island's attractions

For today's visitors, however, the traces of the past are a compelling reason for coming to Cyprus. There are ancient Greek and Roman ruins at Kourion and Salamis, splendid Roman mosaics at Pafos, Crusader castles at Kolossi and atop the Pentadaktylos Mountains, and Byzantine monasteries and churches of the Troödos Mountains.

THE LIE OF THE LAND

Tucked into the extreme eastern corner of the Mediterranean between Turkish Anatolia and Syria, Cyprus is the Mediterranean's third-largest island, after Sicily and Sardinia. Its land surface of 9,251 sq km sandwiches the broad Mesaoria Plain between two chains of mountains – the Pentadaktylos range in the northeast and the Troödos in the southwest. Three major rivers, which run dry in summer, originate in the Troödos Mountains: the Pediaios, flowing east to Famagusta Bay; the Kargotis, north to Morfou Bay; and the Kouris, south to Episkopi. The highest peak is Mt Olympos, at 1,952m (6,403ft).

Population: Just over 1.3 million – around 966,000 in the South, including approximately 190,000 foreign residents; around 400,000 in the North, including some 150,000 post-1974 Turkish settlers. That said, numbers in the North of the island are approximate due to a lack of available data and are likely to be significantly higher than are currently available.

Capital: Nicosia (Lefkosia/Lefkoşa): approx. 364,000.

WHAT'S NEW

Cyprus is undergoing a period of development. Architecturally, modern construction is booming, though not all is done with care for its surroudings, with Limassol seeing the most growth. Island-wide restoration projects are preserving Cypriot heritage buildings.

Limassol has also become an international melting pot, with residents from Russia, Ukraine and Israel contributing to its cultural diversity, bringing in more business opportunities and cultural life.

Festival culture is flourishing, with events like Reflect Festival, Limassol International Book Fair and Fengaros Festival attracting global attention and as municipalities compete for the European Capital of Culture 2030 title, 2025's finalist cities (Limassol and Larnaka) are bursting with events.

The island's culinary scene has also evolved offering dishes that honour Cypriot heritage (To Patriko; Tersefanou) and Peruvian flavours (Tocayo; 10 Prevezis, Nicosia, http://cesorogroup.com). Expect higher prices, though, as the cost of living rises.

Cyprus is diversifying its coastline offerings and yachting facilities, with more marinas like Ayia Napa's and a planned Larnaka marina. Meanwhile, in the north, the once-abandoned town of Varosha is now remarkably open, a first since the 1974 invasion, offering a fascinating glimpse into its Cyprus' pre-war era.

Cyprus is a country of great natural beauty. While the most popular resort beaches cater well to holidaymakers happy to lie baking their bodies in serried ranks, the coastline, particularly along the Akamas and Karpaz peninsulas, has enough rugged cliffs and surf-beaten hidden coves to appeal to more adventurous types.

Inland, the Troödos Mountains are a spectacularly verdant realm of hairpin curves and restored forest. Sprinkled like forgotten gems in the interior's landscape, intrepid travellers will come across tiny Byzantine churches, known only to their parishioners for centuries. Today, many of these places of worship are protected by UNESCO and no visit to Cyprus is complete without visiting at least a few of them.

Rural Cypriot life meanders at an ever-gentle pace. Here, villages untouched by tourism nestle among sun-baked olive groves or citrus orchards, while goats and sheep scamper about forgotten medieval ruins. Vineyards climb the hillsides in preparation for the harvest of local wine, and fragrant cypress trees frame a somnolent abbey or the skeleton of an abandoned fortress.

Amphiteatre Bay, Akamas Peninsula

SUSTAINABLE TRAVEL

Cyprus may not have the best reputation for combating pollution in Europe, yet several initiatives have been recognized for their efforts: NGO AKTI Project and Research Centre was applauded in 2025 for its safeguarding of endangered environmental heritage while the Ineia Turtle Museum, the Lara Bay Turtle Conservation Station and BirdLife Cyprus are doing exceptional work in preserving animal and natural habitats. Many hotel resorts are striving to earn the Green Key eco-label, awarded for energy-saving, waste reduction, and water conservation.

Pedestrian walking paths, more bicycle lanes and the expansion of coastal promenades have increased **transport** on foot or bike across the island, and in the old town, local artists have open studios selling traditional, handmade art.

10 Things not to miss

1

2

3

4

5

6

1 PANAGIA TOU ARAKA

One of the island's most celebrated frescoed churches, in Lagoudera village. See page 72.

2 KERYNEIA

The medieval harbour is the most picturesque in Cyprus. See page 84.

3 CYPRUS MUSEUM

A must-see in Nicosia, housing the island's finest collection of archaeological artefacts. See page 39.

4 BUFFAVENTO

Highest of three Lusignan castles in the Pentadaktylos range, this has superb views over half the island. See page 84.

5 AGIA NAPA

Blonde-sand beaches and excellent hotels. See page 57.

6 FAMAGUSTA

The old town, wrapped in Venetian fortifications, holds many Gothic churches now used as mosques. See page 86.

7 KATO PAFOS

Some of the finest Roman mosaics in the east Mediterranean grace this resort. See page 74.

8 KARPAZ PENINSULA

Byzantine monuments, the island's best seafood and superb, deserted beaches make this remote area a winner. See page 37.

9 AGIOS NEOPHYTOS MONASTERY

The highlight here is the frescoed, rock-cut hermitage. See page 80.

10 KOURION

The ancient clifftop city, one of Cyprus' archaeological highlights, offers mosaics and a restored temple. See page 63.

A perfect tour of Cyprus

DAY 1

Larnaka. Hire a car and head into town for the Pierides and Archaeological museums. Stop for lunch along Piyale Paşa, then book a dive for tomorrow over the Zenobia wreck. Drive to your accommodation in Tochni, before dinner in Zygi.

DAY 2

Limassol. Grab a breakfast pastry from a local bakery and head west along the coast to Limassol, swinging by the Medieval Castle and enjoying lunch in the old quarter. Continue to explore Kourion before dinner in Tochni.

DAY 3

Nicosia. Return to Larnaka for your pre-booked mid-morning dive. Afterwards, do lunch near St Lazarus Church, then head to Nicosia to visit the Cyprus and Byzantine museums. Later, cross the Ledras Street checkpoint to explore the Mevlevî Tekke and the Büyük Han in North Nicosia. Return to the southern sector for dinner.

DAY 4

Keryneia. Take your car across at Agios Dometios/Metehan and reach Keryneia waterfront in time for lunch. Then, head up to Bellapais/Beylerbeyi with its Gothic abbey. Overnight in Keryneia or Bellapais.

DAY 5

Karpasia. Head east to Kantara Castle. Lunch at a local fish taverna before a visit to Agias Trias basilica. Stop for a swim at Golden Beach, then overnight in Dipkarpaz (Rizokarpaso). Watch the sunset from Agios Filon/Ayfilon cove.

DAY 6

Three towns. Get an early start to see ancient Salamis and then Famagusta before lunch. Visit Varosha's "ghost town". Use the Pergamos/Pyla checkpoint and spend the night in Oroklini.

DAY 7

Troödos painted churches. Take the Larnaca-Nicosia highway towards the mountains. Visit Agios Nikolaos tis Stegis church and walk Kakopetria's alleys and nature trails. Have lunch in Kalopanagiotis, visiting the Agios Lampadistes Ioannis Monastery, then drive up to your base at Pano Platres.

DAY 8

To Pafos. Leave Pano Platres via a Limassol winery, then change valleys for lunch at Ariadne's, outside Vasa. A lovely route leads quickly downhill, via Koulkia and Palaia Paphos, to Pafos. Dine al fresco at 7 St Georges taverna, before an overnight stay in Pafos.

DAY 9

Around Pafos. Spend the morning at Pafos Mosaics, then St Neophytos. After lunch at Laona, head to the turtle beach of Lara. Dinner is on the terrace at Imogen's in Kathikas. Overnight in Pafos before your flight home.

Beach hopping in Protaras

DAY 1

Cape Gkreko. Konnos Bay offers watersports, a shaded café, and facilities. Spend the day here, making time to visit nearby Ayioi Anargiroi chapel for panoramic views. Descend the cliff stairs for a swim before heading to Cape Gkreko for an epic sunset. Note: rent a car or motorbike for this trip. Take a late dinner after sundown.

DAY 2

Green Bay. A popular diving and watersports hub with ample parking near Cavo Maris Hotel. Rent SUPs or jet skis (www.greenbaywake.com), then walk to a café for lunch. Close by, Vyzakia Beach has great snorkelling. Stay until the sun sets and the crowds disperse. See page 91.

DAY 3

Fig Tree Bay. The best blue-flag beach in central Protaras. Arrive early to make the most of it before the crowds pour in and stay here to soak up the rays all day. Tip: swim out to the small island for some excellent snorkelling.

DAY 4

Pernera. This is a family-friendly bay with shallow waters and sunbeds. A coastal walking path and parking are nearby. Bonus tip: snorkel to spot a sculpture of a female underwater.

DAY 5

Golden Coast. Named after the adjacent hotel, there are sunbeds, umbrellas and nearby fish tavernas. Rest, re-apply your sunscreen and visit the picturesque chapel of Agios Nikolaos.

DAY 6

Vrysoudi Beach. Away from the tourist centre, this beach has a grassy area with a summer café-bar and fish taverna, ample parking, too.

DAY 7

Agia Triada. A small harbour and quaint chapel enclose this sandy beach. Each summer, caretta-caretta turtles frequent the surrounding rocks – locals will often point them out.

DAY 8

Pezounospylies. Explore this secluded beach – free of municipal sunbeds. Tucked between the cliffs near the Green Line, it's accessed via a dirt road past Kapparis beach and down a steep wooden staircase. It has a pebbly shore with stunning caves and is a great snorkelling spot.

DAY 9

Ammos tou Kambouri. Near Agia Napa's hotel district, this quiet sandy beach has sunbeds with cushions and straw umbrellas. Rocks in the water may limit swimming. Or take the coast path to nearby shores.

DAY 10

Nissi Beach. This Blue Flag beach boasts soft sand, clear waters and ample space for sunbathers, beach volleyball and swimmers.

A perfect day in Nicosia

9AM

Breakfast. Enjoy a classic Cypriot breakfast at Tria Fanaria (22 664706, @TriaFanaria) in front of Faneromenis School – try a *tiropitta* (cheese pie), spinach pie, or a flaky almond croissant.

10AM

Old town stroll. Explore Ledra Street and Laiki Geitonia, browsing local shops on your way to the Leventis Museum, which offers a deep dive into Nicosia's history. Check for temporary exhibitions while you're there and browse its excellent shop.

12.30PM

Lunch. For a truly Cypriot meal, head to Evroulla (22 665346, @evroulla_traditional_kitchen) in Stoa Klokkari. This small eatery serves hand-cut fries, grilled halloumi, bean stew, souvlaki, and village salad.

2PM

Cross the checkpoint. Make your way down Onasagorou Street to the Ledras Street checkpoint into northern Nicosia. Visit Büyük Han, an Ottoman-era inn now hosting art shops and cafés. Behind it is Selimiye Camii, a former Gothic church turned mosque. Turn onto Selimiye Sokak where shops sell Turkish-style lamps, evil eye charms and mosaic plates.

4.30PM

Coffee stop. Cross back into southern Nicosia for a coffee break at Giagia Victoria (22 777252) to the right next to the checkpoint, hidden by barricades of the Green Line. Pair a traditional coffee, with *bougatsa*, *galaktoboureko* (filo pastry dessert with syrup) or an orange pie.

5.30PM

Museum hopping. Head to the Nicosia Municipal Arts Centre for contemporary art and check out the Nicosia Town Hall (www.nicosia.org.cy) opposite – a glass, wood and steel building that sits above archaeological finds. Nearby are the Archbishop's Palace, a grandiose building you can only admire from the outside, and quaint Agios Ioannis church next door.

6.30PM

Landmarks. Adjacent are the Cyprus Folk Art Museum and the National Struggle Museum (though they close early) and opposite stands the neo-classical Pancyprian Gymnasium, Cyprus' oldest high school and an architectural marvel. Within the old town's Venetian walls, stop to see Famagusta Gate.

8PM

Meze dinner. Head to Zanettos Tavern, near Ömeriye Mosque for a meze dinner. Allow a few hours here.

10PM

Brandy sour. End the night with the island's signature cocktail, the brandy sour, a lemony drink made with angostura bitters. Yiamas!

History

A crossing point between the three continents – Europe, Asia and Africa – Cyprus has historically had a troublesome past, passed from invader to invader. Yet its presence on the map appeared long before its kingdoms and battles.

The first humans on Cyprus were nomads and hunters rather than permanently settled groups. Flint tools discovered offshore from the Akamas Peninsula and on Nissi Beach at Agia Napa prove that seafarers landed on Cyprus in about 10,000 BC. The bones of indigenous pygmy hippopotamuses and pygmy elephants (both now extinct) eaten by the mariners were also found. Tools and butchered animal bones found in a coastal cave at Akrotiri date from about 9000 BC. The earliest traces of permanent settlers date from about 8000 BC, the most notable being the stone beehive-shaped dwellings at the tip of the Karpaz Peninsula and at the inland sites of Choroiditis (Khirokitía) and Tenta (Ténda).

Original mosaic of Leda and the Swan, Palaipaphos Museum

By 3500 BC, copper was being mined in the Troödos foothills and Cyprus began to prosper as a trading centre, with goods arriving from Asia, Egypt, Crete, the Peloponnese and the Aegean islands in exchange for Cypriot pottery, copperware and opium. After 1600 BC, fortresses appear, which suggests a period of insecurity and outside threats.

Greeks, Persians and Romans

Climactic and demographic upheaval in the Peloponnese drove Mycenaean Greeks east across the Mediterranean, and some settled in Cyprus. Around 1200 BC, they established city-kingdoms at Enkomi/Alasia Salamis (near modern Famagusta), Marion (near Polis), Tamassos, Kition (now Larnaka), Kourion, Palaia Pafos (modern Kouklia), Soloi and Lapethos. The island acquired the predominantly Greek identity it was never entirely to relinquish.

As the Persian Empire spread across the eastern Mediterranean in the sixth century BC, Cyprus, along with other Greek islands, was annexed. In 499 BC it joined the Ionian Greek revolt but, after heroic resistance, notably during the sieges of Soloi and Palaia Pafos, was crushed by the Persians the next year.

In 333 BC, Alexander the Great ended Persian dominance in the eastern Mediterranean and placed Cyprus under Macedonian rule. After his death in 323 BC, his generals fought over the succession, flattening many Cypriot cities in the process. By 294 BC, Ptolemy I emerged the victor, the city-kingdoms disappeared and Cyprus became part of Hellenistic Egypt. The Ptolemies ruled for 250 years until the Romans annexed it in 58 BC to their province of Cilicia (southern Turkey).

In 47 BC, Julius Caesar made a present of Cyprus to Cleopatra, the last Ptolemaic ruler. After her suicide, Augustus took it back for the Romans and let King Herod of Judaea farm out the Cypriot copper mines to Jewish entrepreneurs.

The Byzantine Era

Despite the apostle Paul's mission to Cyprus in AD 45, most islanders continued to be devoutly pagan, though not Jewish – all Jews were expelled by Emperor Hadrian after a bloody revolt in AD

116. Only during the fourth century, as Christianity spread to the Roman leadership, did churches and monasteries multiply across Cyprus. In AD 330, the mother of Roman emperor Constantine, Helena, supposedly visited the island and founded the great Stavrovouni Monastery.

In 488, when the relics of Barnabas (Paul's evangelizing companion) were miraculously found, the Church of Cyprus became autonomous, subject only to Constantinople, and not nearby Antioch or Jerusalem. The archbishop of Cyprus could carry a royal sceptre rather than a pastoral staff, wear a cloak of imperial purple and sign his name in imperial red ink – rights that the archbishops retain to this day.

With the Byzantine Empire weakened by war against Persia, the Arabs took the opportunity to attack Cyprus in 649 with a fleet of 1,500 ships. Salamis (now Constantia) was left in such ruins that it never recovered.

Four years later, in a move that foreshadowed events of the twentieth century, the Arabs staged a second invasion and left a garrison of 12,000 men, encouraging Muslim civilian immigration. The Byzantines and the Caliphate subsequently agreed to demilitarize Cyprus and also to share tax revenues. Over the next three hundred years, Muslims and Christians engaged in offshore battles, but lived side by side.

The Crusades and the Lusignans

During the Crusades, Cyprus became a key strategic post for Byzantine interests in Syria and Palestine. The governor organized protection for pilgrims to the Holy Land and supervised the rebuilding of Jerusalem's Church of the Holy Sepulchre and fortifications for its Christian Quarter. The invasion of Seljuk Turks in Anatolia and the Levant after 1071 threatened communications with Constantinople, but Cyprus was still able to supply soldiers of the First Crusade in 1097 and even provided refuge for defeated Muslim princes.

New trade developed with Venice and the young Crusader states on the mainland. However, the Seljuks' domination of Anatolia after 1176 isolated Cyprus from the Byzantine government. Isaac Komnenos, a junior member of the imperial family, declared himself 'Emperor' of Cyprus in 1184.

Stavrovouni Monastery mosaic

Deliverance from his greedy, brutal rule came in the form of England's King Richard the Lionheart, who anchored at Limassol en route to the Third Crusade. After a brief campaign, he defeated and imprisoned Komnenos, then promptly sold the island to the Knights Templar. Their greed prompted another revolt which they could not quell, and the island returned briefly to Richard's suzerainty before being acquired by Guy de Lusignan, a French former king of Jerusalem. In 1260, the Roman Catholic Church was declared supreme on the island, with Orthodox bishops rusticated to remote hill villages.

Genoese and Venetians

During the fourteenth century, Cyprus shone as the easternmost Christian outpost, now that the Holy Land was permanently lost. Famagusta's merchants in particular became renowned for their extravagant wealth. The island's opulence attracted pirates, and fuelled a heated rivalry between Venetian and Genoese merchants that erupted in bloody riots in late 1372. The Cypriots sided with

Othello's Tower, Famagusta

the Lusignans and Venetians against the Genoese, murdering merchants and looting shops in Famagusta. In retaliation, Genoa sent a fleet to ravage the island, seizing Famagusta in late 1373.

Worse followed in 1425, when the Mamelukes landed on the south coast, defeated King Janus, and rendered him a vassal of Egypt. Successor King James II was only able to oust the Genoese from Famagusta in 1464 with Egyptian funding, but it was too late to restore Lusignan power. He married a Venetian noblewoman, Caterina Cornaro, and then died (probably of Venetian poisoning); the Venetian then forced Queen Caterina to abdicate, and ruled Cyprus directly for the next 82 years.

The Venetians' lucrative trade routes were threatened by Ottoman encroachment on three sides – Anatolia, the Levant and Egypt. The Turks landed on the south coast mid-1570 and took Nicosia after a 46-day siege. The capital's Venetian commander was killed and his head sent as a warning to Marcantonio Bragadino, commander at Famagusta. Undeterred, Bragadino led a heroic defence, with 8,000 Greek-Cypriot and Italian troops holding out for over ten months against a Turkish army of two hundred thousand. On 1 August 1571, his ammunition gone, Bragadino surrendered. He was promised safe passage, but when Ottoman commander Lala Mustapha Pasha saw he had lost fifty thousand men to such a tiny army, he flayed Bragadino alive. Cyprus was now a province of the Ottoman Empire.

Ottoman rule

With the Turks controlling the whole of the eastern Mediterranean, Cyprus lost its strategic importance and was left to stagnate. Venetians converted to Islam, and soldiers and their families, plus civilian settlers from Anatolia, were the forerunners of today's Turkish-Cypriot community. Most Greek Cypriots, who had loathed the Venetians, initially welcomed Ottoman rule, especially when the Orthodox Church was restored to supremacy. By 1660, the Sultan officially recognized the Greek Orthodox archbishop as the head of the Greek Cypriot community.

At the beginning of the Greek War of Independence of 1821, the local Ottoman governor executed charismatic Archbishop Kyprianos, including his three bishops and hundreds of prominent civilians, which as a result provoked 12 subsequent years of revolt, which was met with massacre and plunder by Syrian and Egyptian troops.

Over the subsequent decades, the Sultan attempted to halt widespread abuses by tax collectors, which were provoking massive emigration of both Greek and Turkish Cypriots. But local officials opposed all of these reforms. The disintegration of the Ottoman authority in Cyprus was symptomatic of the progressive collapse of the empire.

The British step in

Great Britain spent the mid-nineteenth century fending off Russian initiatives to seize Ottoman territory; finally, in 1878, in consideration of services rendered to the Ottomans in the most recent Russo-Turkish war, occupation and administration of Cyprus (though not formal sovereignty) was ceded to Britain. Once Britain acquired nearby Egypt and its Suez Canal in 1882, Cyprus' importance was reinforced.

Greek Cypriots were initially happy about the transfer of power, and came to appreciate the new schools, hospitals, law courts, aqueducts and roads furnished by British colonial administration. But they primarily expected the British to help Cyprus achieve *enosis*, or union with Greece, as Britain had done for the Ionian Islands in 1864.

Union with Greece was, of course, opposed by the Turkish-Cypriots. They remained confident that Britain would respect its treaty with Turkey and not give in to demands for *enosis*. In 1914, Turkey sided with the Central Powers in World War I and Britain promptly annexed Cyprus, making it a British Crown Colony. In 1931, Greek-Cypriot members of the Legislative Council resigned, and riots broke out in Nicosia. The British response was harsh: reparations for damages, declaration of martial law, the banning of political parties and display of the Greek flag, deportation of troublemakers.

The fight for enosis

In 1947, the local British governor offered limited self-rule to Cyprus, as with other colonies at the time. But the Greek-Cypriot slogan of the day was '*enosis* and only *enosis*'. In 1950 a plebiscite of Greek Cypriots voted 96 percent in favour of union with Greece, a vote overseen by the local church's new leader, Archbishop Makarios III (see box).

In 1955, the campaign for *enosis* became violent, led by Colonel (later General) Georgios Grivas, a Cypriot-born Greek Army officer. Directed from a hideout deep in the Troödos Mountains, EOKA (the Greek initials for the National Organisation of Cypriot Fighters) bombed public buildings and assassinated opponents of *enosis*. Archbishop Makarios publicly disowned the actions, but gave EOKA clandestine support. He was exiled in 1956, first to the Seychelles and then to Athens. In Greece itself both the government and the public gave noisy support to the Greek-Cypriot cause, which only irritated Turkey.

Turkey opposed *enosis* with two main arguments: the Turkish-Cypriot community would be defenceless if it was swallowed up in

Venetian-era Keryneia Castle

the greater Greek nation; and Greek territorial extension to Cyprus would pose a military threat to Turkey. In 1958, some Turkish Cypriots founded the organization TMT to work, violently if necessary, for partition of the island.

In 1959, the foreign ministers of Turkey and Greece, plus, later, British figures and representatives of both Greek and Turkish Cypriots, met in Zurich and London. As a result, all parties agreed to renounce either *enosis* or partition, while guaranteeing safeguards to protect the Turkish-Cypriot minority in a new independent republic. The first president of the republic would be Greek-Cypriot Archbishop Makarios, and his vice-president would be the Turkish-Cypriot leader Fazil Küçük. On 16 August 1960, Cyprus became independent, though Britain retained two large military bases on the south coast.

A SMALL NATION'S GREAT LEADER

The first president of Cyprus was the Pafos-born Archbishop Makarios who first was a monk at Kykkos Monastery and then Bishop of Kition (Larnaka) following studies in Athens, Istanbul and Boston.

Made archbishop at the young age of 37, he won popular support with his dignified eloquence. But he was criticized by foreign observers for his failure to control Greek-Cypriot extremists, thus provoking alarm among Turkish Cypriots. Makarios, who died in 1977, impressed the world with his moral leadership of non-aligned nations at the height of the Cold War, and his courage during the Greek-inspired coup against him in 1974 and the subsequent Turkish invasion.

Troubled independence

Cabinet posts, parliamentary seats and civil service jobs were apportioned to Greek and Turkish Cypriots according to a 70:30 ratio, and the main towns elected separate Greek- and Turkish-Cypriot municipal governments, but the constitution proved unworkably complex. In late 1963, Makarios proposed thirteen simplifying amendments which the Turkish Cypriots refused; fighting soon broke out in Nicosia. The British supervised a cease-fire and set up a 'Green Line' (see box) separating the communities. United Nations forces were brought in to patrol the Green Line in March 1964, and they have stayed ever since. All Turkish Cypriots left their government posts on TMT orders, and many Turkish Cypriots from mixed villages sought shelter in fortified enclaves, which sprang up across the island. Turkey and Greece each supplemented their existing island garrisons with more officers sent to train local forces. Among them was General Grivas, in 1971, who took control of far-rightist EOKA-B (EOKA the Second). Continual attempts to reconcile the two island communities were sabotaged by outside parties, including the military junta in control of Greece since 1967.

On 15 July 1974, Greece's junta tried to impose *enosis* on Cyprus through a coup mounted by EOKA-B. The Presidential Palace was attacked, although Makarios escaped to Pafos and refuted reports of his demise with a radio broadcast. Although the illegitimate regime collapsed within eight days, the coup d'état gave Turkey a pretext to invade on 20 July. The Greek Cypriots, weakened by an ongoing civil war between leftists and EOKA-B, stood little chance, and by 14 August Turkish troops had occupied northern Cyprus. Makarios escaped to New York, where he rallied support in the UN to reinstate him as president. The Turkish army remained in control of 38 percent of the island, including Famagusta, northern Nicosia and Keryneia. Some 180,000 Greek Cypriots were forced to flee to the south, while about 44,000 Turkish Cypriots migrated to the north. By 2005, approximately eighty thousand settlers had been sent to northern Cyprus from Turkey.

Archbishop Makarios (1913–1977), first President of Cyprus

In 1983, the so-called Turkish Republic of Northern Cyprus (recognized only by Turkey) was set up with Rauf Denktash as president. The UN condemned the move and urged the leaders to find a way other than partition to protect minority rights on the island. Due to the diplomatic isolation of the north, the economy there stagnated. The Greek Cypriot economy, on the other hand, recovered quickly from the shock of invasion, helped both by tourism and – represented by the only 'legitimate' government on the island – international aid.

Successive rounds of UN-sponsored negotiations between Denktash and the incumbent Greek Cypriot president, from 1981 onwards, got nowhere, largely thanks to Denktash's obstructionism and post-Makarios President Spyros Kyprianou's timidity. Much of the 1990s were spent in arms build-ups on both sides, border incidents and mutual threats.

The oppressive rule of Denktash and his UBP party, coupled with a Turkish economic crash which dragged the North down with it, caused the first serious Turkish-Cypriot opposition to the status quo during 2000–1, with demonstrations and renewed intercommunal initiatives. Denktash, under continued domestic pressure, abruptly opened the Ledra Palace crossing of the Green Line in April 2003, allowing native Cypriots on both sides almost unconditional access to the other. Since then, eight other automobile or pedestrian crossings – including the highly symbolic Ledra Street/Lokmacı one in central Nicosia – have opened.

Cyprus joined the EU in 2004

Cyprus in the EU

In tandem with Cyprus' pending EU membership

THE GREEN LINE

The Green Line owes its name to the British army officer who drew a line in green crayon on a map to separate the warring Greek and Turkish Cypriot communities in Nicosia. Since 1974, the ceasefire line has extended across the entire island; outside the city it is generally known as the Attila Line, after the Turks' own code designation for their invasion. Either side of the line is a 'dead zone' (buffer zone), usually heavily mined, varying in width from a few metres in central Nicosia to a kilometre or so in sensitive areas. The line can now be crossed in either direction at one of nine authorized points, by native Greek or Turkish Cypriots, and all EU nationals. This is a marked contrast to the conditions that prevailed before April 2003, when only non-Cypriot visitors could transit from the South to the North on foot, with return stipulated by nightfall.

on 1 May 2004, the UN presented yet another federal settlement proposal: the (Kofi) Annan Plan. Upon approval via referendum, the entire island would join the EU. The plan – conceding a huge role to Turkey – was approved 2:1 by Turkish Cypriots, but rejected 3:1 by Greek Cypriots. Two decades later, the UN's patience has worn thin, with a warning that the plan can only be minimally modified.

Later, the importance of a settlement receded for Greek Cypriots preoccupied with the 2013 economic crisis in the South. The two largest banks were effectively bankrupt and tourism proceeds were sharply down. The winner of the 2013 presidential elections, DISY (centre-right) party chief Nicos Anastasiades, had to apply for a €16 billion EU bailout to keep Cyprus going. Uproar ensued as the Cypriot parliament rejected the German-led 'troïka' deal; finally, on 25 March 2013, a package expropriating almost 40 percent of deposits over the guarantee limit was agreed, ending Cyprus' long-running offshore banking enterprise. The only hope of repaying the €10 billion troïka loan lies in undersea natural gas fields which Cyprus is preparing to exploit with Israel. In 2020, Greece, Cyprus and Israel signed a deal to build a pipeline to carry natural gas to Europe, despite opposition from Turkey – the latest in a long line of disputes over sea boundaries in the eastern Mediterranean.

UN watchtower on the border, Nicosia

High hopes for reunification

In 2014 the President of the Republic of Cyprus, Nicos Anastasiades, and his Northern Cyprus compatriot Derviş Eroğlu relaunched negotiations to settle the Cyprus dispute. Talks reached stalemate but there was new hope in May 2015 when Mustafa Akıncı became the new president of Northern Cyprus. Talks resumed, resulting in Northern Cyprus lifting visa requirements for Greek Cypriots.

However, resolution appeared to be slipping further away following the election of anti-reunification nationalist Ersin Tatar as President of the Turkish Republic of Northern Cyprus in October 2020. UN troops continue to guard the Green Line which divides the two parts of the island.

Rise of the far right

In May 2021, Cyprus' ruling centre-right Democratic Rally clung to its top spot in the country's parliamentary election, though it lost significant ground amid corruption allegations. The election campaign was marred by Cyprus' so-called "golden visa" cash-for-passports scheme, after news reports revealed high-ranking officials, politicians and lawyers were willing to help convicted criminals obtain citizenship through the scheme. This controversy sparked the rise of the far-right Elam party, which made the most substantial gains in the election. While the Democratic Party had its worst result in forty years, Elam doubled its support, jumping from seventh to fourth place, after the communist Akel party and centrist Diko party.

Caught in the middle

Between 2022 and 2024, refugees and asylum seekers from Africa and Syria arrived at the island's shores at a staggering rate. Cyprus struggled to handle this migration influx with reception centres quickly overfilling. To handle it, the government tightened asylum regulations and accelerated deportation – actions that sparked criticism from human rights organizations.

The management of the Mediterranean refugee crisis was a big part of Nikos Christodoulides' presidential campaign – he was elected in 2023. His neutral stance to the neighbouring Israel-Palestine conflict from 2024 was also criticised, as Cyprus' foreign bases in RAF Akrotiri were used for strategic military and intelligence operations, sparking outcry with the Cypriot public who protested.

Christodoulides' presidency signaled a cautious optimism to reignite reunification talks without any practical success apart from returning to peace talks in Geneva in early 2025 along with the Turkish-Cypriot leader, Ersin Tatar.

Chronology

c.10,000 BC First evidence of human occupation.
c.8000 BC First permanent settlements on Cyprus.
c.3500 BC Copper mines in Troödos foothills establish early wealth.
1200 BC Mycenaean Greeks settle on the island.

333 BC Alexander the Great expels Persians.
294 BC Cyprus subject to Hellenistic Egypt under the Ptolemy dynasty.
58 BC Romans annexe Cyprus to their empire.
4th century AD Christianity takes hold; many churches built.
649–53 Arabs invade and settle on the island.
963–1184 Middle Byzantine period. Cyprus flourishes.
1191–92 England's Richard the Lionheart defeats Isaac Komnenos and sells Cyprus to Guy de Lusignan, who founds a 300-year dynasty.
1489 Venetians depose the last Lusignan ruler, Caterina Cornaro.
1571 Fall of Famagusta to the Turks ends Venetian rule.
1571–1878 Period of Ottoman rule.
1878 Cyprus occupied by Britain, with Ottoman agreement.
1914 Ottomans back Central Powers in World War I; Britain takes Cyprus.
1955 EOKA begins campaign of violence in pursuit of enosis.
1959–60 Independence negotiated and granted.
1963–64 Intercommunal strife endangers young republic; UN intervenes.
1974 Coup by Greek military junta gives Turkey pretext to invade.
1983 The 'Turkish Republic of Northern Cyprus' is declared by the North.
2003 De facto border between South and North opened to free transit.
2004 The Republic of Cyprus joins the EU without Northern Cyprus.
2008 The euro is introduced in the South.
2013 Economic crisis overtakes the South; EU aid package sees €5.8 billion seized from high-value bank accounts.
2015 Talks on Cyprus reunification resume.
2016 President Anastasiades and Turkish Cypriot leader Mustafa Akinci make a joint New Year television address.
2018 Nicos Anastasiades is re-elected President of Cyprus for a second term.

2020 The Covid-19 pandemic spreads across the world. Ersin Tatar becomes the President of Northern Cyprus.
2021 In May, the Democratic Rally party wins the Cypriot parliamentary election. In December, Pope Francis pays an apostolic visit to Cyprus.
2022 Tourism slowly returns to boost the economy.
2023 Nikos Christodoulides is elected president of the Republic.
2024 Cyprus to join the Schengen Zone by end 2025, aiming to enhance European integration and facilitate travel.
2025 UN-backed peace talks in Geneva report meaningful progress, with both Cypriot sides agreeing to open new crossing points and initiate confidence-building measures.

President Nikos Christodoulides at an EU Summit in Brussels

Clear waters near Agia Napa

Places

If you really want to get to know Cyprus, and not just soak up the sun on the island's alluring beaches, you should aim to stay in more than one place. If you're based at one of its southern extremities – Pafos or Agia Napa – spend a few nights at a more central coastal location around Limassol, or to go inland to Nicosia or the Troödos Mountains. You may also want to set aside time for the North, where the best overnight options are around Keryneia or on the Karpaz Peninsula.

Nicosia and environs

Highlights

Nicosia (*Lefkosia* in Greek, *Lefkoşa* in Turkish) ❶ is Cyprus' only major city in the interior, occupying the site of ancient Ledra, founded in the third century BC by Lefkonas, son of Ptolemy I of Egypt. When coastal Paphos and Salamis (Constantia) came under Arab attack during the seventh century AD, the population moved inland and Nicosia became the chief city. Under the Lusignans, it grew into a splendid capital marked by elegant churches and monasteries in the French Gothic style.

Almost everything of interest to travellers lies within, or just outside, the old city walls. The ramparts, built by the Venetians in preparation for the Turkish invasion of 1570, remain Nicosia's dominant feature. The wheel-shaped Renaissance fortification has become the modern capital's distinctive logo, with its eleven-pointed bastions and three gateways named after the coastal cities to which they lead – Famagusta Gate to the east, Pafos Gate to the west and Keryneia (Girne) Gate to the north. Some of the bastions now shelter municipal offices, while sections of the (now dry) moat serve as public gardens, seasonal fun fair and concert grounds as well as car parks.

Since the Turkish invasion of 1974, Nicosia remains a divided city, roughly half in Southern Cyprus, half in the North; the 'Green Line' buffer zone that straddles the dividing line, with its derelict 1930s buildings, UN, Greek-Cypriot and Turkish-Cypriot checkpoints, barbed wire, sandbags and roadblocks, is an eerie reminder of this.

WHERE TO SHOOT THE BEST PICTURES

Buffavento castle Possibly the island's most scenic landscape views lay here. It's a trek to the top but totally worth it – especially at dusk and dawn. Try to frame the tower's window with a back-drop of the mountains.

Avakas gorge Squat down and tilt your camera upwards to get both sides of the gorge in their tall, red-brown glory. If you're using a phone, turn it upside down with the camera on the bottom side for elongated pics.

Pafos Lighthouse Once past the mosaics, keep walking until you see the white Lighthouse; it's a particularly picturesque sight especially in spring when the fields are green and yellow daisies and red poppies grow.

Nicosia Tahtakale and Chrysaliniotissa For a perfect postcard of the capital city stroll this neighbourhood and capture the many friendly cats sleeping on window ledges of old mansions.

Sea Caves Carefully climb down the Cape Gkreko Sea Caves to find a round, hollow rock overlooking the bright blue waters. Newlyweds even venture down for a unique picture here for its breathtaking natural frame. Avoid when windy or when the tide is high though.

However, the Cypriot capital is experiencing something of a rebirth. Both tourists and Cypriots can now pass with relative ease; visitors on foot typically use the Ledra/Lokmacı and Ledra Palace crossings, though you can walk through Agios Dometios or Pyla if you are being collected by a car or person the other side.

The rich café culture in Nicosia

Many visitors spend just a day here, but an overnight stay (or more) is well worthwhile if you want to explore both halves of the fortified city properly – and experience some of the best dining opportunities on the island. Be prepared for real summer heat – Nicosia is around three or four degrees hotter than the coast, with temperatures soaring to 37°C (99°F) in July.

The Cyprus Museum

The island's finest collection of antiquities is housed in the **Cyprus Museum** Ⓐ (22865854; free) on 1 Miki Theodoraki Avenue (previously known as and still come across on some maps as Mouseiou), just west of the walled city near the Pafos Gate. The neoclassical building houses archaeological artefacts dating from the Stone Age (around 8000 BC) to the Roman era, though the most riveting displays are of Bronze Age and Archaic vintage. Plans for a new purpose-built annexe linked to the existing building by an underpass or aerial bridge are underway yet the grand opening will likely take time. The guards may proudly tell you that the items in storage could fill four museums.

Exhibits from the early Bronze Age, in Room 2, include the so-called sanctuary model (2000 BC), in which worshippers and priests attend a bull sacrifice while a peeping Tom on the sanctuary wall watches the secret ceremony. In Room 3, an intriguing Mycenaean *krater* (drinking cup) imported to Enkomi in the fourteenth century BC has an octopus motif framing a scene of Zeus preparing warriors for battle at Troy; nearby, a beautiful green faïence *rhyton* (ritual drinking vessel) of the twelfth century BC depicts a lively bull-hunt in Kition.

Room 5 has a rich collection of sculpture, and the highlight is a trio of magnificent lions, tongues and teeth bared, plus two sphinxes, discovered in 1997 guarding tombs at Tamassos. Left of these is a double-sided limestone stele depicting Dionysos on one side, and on the other, facing the wall, an erotic scene leaving nothing to the imagination. At the far end of the hall, a sensuous marble Aphrodite has become the logo of island tourism despite having lost her arms and lower legs.

Statue of Aphrodite

The monumental bronze of Roman Emperor Septimius Severus (*c.*AD 200) dominates Room 6, among other marble and bronze sculptures. Highlights of Room 7

CYPRUS' TERRACOTTA ARMY

Perhaps the most memorable exhibit in the Cyprus Museum is the 'Terracotta Army', consisting of over five hundred votive statues and figurines dating from between 625 and 500 BC (an equal number were taken to Stockholm by the Swedish excavators). Found at Agia Irini in northwest Cyprus, the figurines are displayed as they originally stood, around the altar of an open-air sanctuary dedicated to a dual cult of war and fertility. Soldiers, war chariots, priests with bull masks, sphinxes, minotaurs and bulls were fashioned in all sizes, from life-size to just 10cm (4ins) tall, and at various levels of workmanship, according to the wealth of the donor.

include the 'Horned God' from Enkomi, one hand downturned in a blessing gesture, and gold pieces from the Lambousa Treasure Hoard. Up short stairs in Room 11 is some fascinating royal tomb furniture from Salamis (eighth century BC): an ivory throne, a bed, ornamentation for two funerary chariots and their horses' tackle.

Along Odos Lidras

The old city's principal thoroughfare and main pedestrianized shopping street, **Ledras**, runs north from Plateia Eleftherias to the Ledra/Lokmacı crossing. Just off its southern end, at Ippokratous 17, stands the award-winning **Leventis Municipal Museum of Nicosia** **B** (www.leventismuseum.org.cy; free), three floors of a fine nineteenth-century neoclassical mansion devoted to the city's history as reflected in privately donated archaeological collections, Lusignan pottery, metal utensils, old engravings and posters, displays on trades or crafts, and worthwhile temporary exhibitions.

Just east of the museum spreads the so-called **Laïki Geitonia** (Traditional Pedestrian Neighbourhood), which purports to recreate old Nicosia. Various buildings in traditional style – some restored, others purpose-built – house galleries, cafés and tavernas. In short, it's a bit of a tourist trap.

Church of Panagia Chrysaliniotissa, Nicosia

Slightly further up Lidras, the Shacolas Tower Museum & Observatory (22674139; charge) is located on the top floor of the sixth-tallest building in Nicosia. The first five floors are occupied by an H&M store – bypass these and head instead to the museum and observatory on the top floor for excellent views of the whole city. The 'museum' bit is rather bogus, though, consisting merely of poor reproductions of archival photos.

East of, and parallel to, Lidras is pedestrianized Onasagorou, less chain-store dominated and with interesting restaurants and cafés. It leads north to the landmark church of **Panagia Faneromeni Church**, dating from 1872 in its present form and the last resting place of four bishops executed in 1821. Nearby is the chunky but handsome **Araplar Mosque**, usually closed to the public, converted into its current guise from the former sixteenth-century church of Stavros tou Missirikou.

The Archbishop's Palace and around

Linchpin of eastern Greek Cypriot old Nicosia is the **Archbishop's Palace** on Plateia Archiepiskopou Kyprianou, a grandiose pastiche built during the 1980s to replace its predecessor, destroyed by EOKA-B during its July 1974 putsch. The only portions of it generally open to the public, at the rear right as you face it, are the **Byzantine**

Museum and Art Galleries Ⓒ (www.makariosfoundation.org.cy; charge) which were renovated in 2025. The upper storey, with its second-rate collection of religious paintings is distinctly optional, but the ground-floor galleries are essential viewing. Here you'll find superb icons rescued from all over Cyprus, though the main stars are towards the rear. Don't miss the display of seven splendid sixth-century mosaics from Panagia Kanakaria church in Northern Cyprus, recovered through court action during the 1980s and 1990s after they were looted and put up for sale on the international art market. Immediately adjacent are the best fifteenth-century frescoes from Antiphonitis Monastery in the North, reclaimed in 1997 after having been similarly looted and illegally exported. In another corner is more recently repatriated art: magnificent thirteenth-century frescoes from the chapel of Agios Evfimianos at Lysi in the North, comprising a Christ Pandokrator in a dome, and a Virgin flanked by angels in an apse, remounted exactly as they were in their original setting.

Next to this museum is **Agios Ioannis** (22 554600), Nicosia's small Orthodox cathedral, built in 1662 in an approximation of Late Gothic style on the site of a former Lusignan Benedictine monastery. Its colourful eighteenth-century frescoes depict key moments in the island's early Christian history. The adjacent Gothic-arcaded

NOTES

Most visitors to the old city enter via Plateia Eleftherias, a prominent square just south-west of the walled city. The multi-level design by Zaha Hadid Architects (ZHA) was finally completed in 2021 and comprises of a series of tree-shaded promenades, paved plazas and water features built into the dry moat. Right by the walls of the D'Avila Bastion are patches of green, a few cafés and an outdoor amphitheatre where events are sometimes held. If you follow it to the end, you'll reach the D'Avila Bastion car park.

building, all that remains of the thirteenth-century monastery, is now the **Cyprus Folk Art Museum** (www.cypriotstudies.org; charge), also called the Ethnographic Museum, full of wooden water wheels, looms, pottery, carved and painted bridal chests, lace, embroidered costumes and much else besides.

Next door the **National Struggle Museum** (22305878; free), minimally labelled in English – it's meant mostly for Greek Cypriot schoolchildren – glorifies EOKA's campaign of shootings, sabotage and demonstrations, as well as documenting the harsh British reprisals. Displays include cartoons, witty graffiti, newspaper clippings, final letters of condemned prisoners and EOKA fighters' belongings.

Immediately west of the Cyprus Folk Art Museum along Palias Ilektrikis stands the **Nicosia Municipal Arts Centre** **D** (www.nimac.org.cy; free), the city's primary modern-art museum, universally known as the Palia Ilektriki ('Old Electric') from its being a converted power plant. The centre focuses on promoting fine arts and its constantly changing exhibits are generally compelling, plus there's a cocktail bar on the premises.

To experience a more successful rejuvenation project than Laïki Geitonia, it's worth strolling from the vicinity of the Archbishop's Palace towards the far northeasterly corner of the Greek-Cypriot old town. Here, the contiguous neighbourhoods of **Tahtakale** (with a fine old mosque) and **Chrysaliniotissa** (Khrysaliniotissa) have had their Ottoman-era mansions and humbler houses repaired and painted in a varied palette, and their interiors renovated to serve as housing for families. Heart of the latter district is the originally Lusignan church of **Panagia Chrysaliniotissa Church** **E** (Our Lady of the Golden Flax). First thought to be built in 1450, it is rarely open unless there is a service, but the finely carved exterior is the main attraction, with most of its interior art now safely in the Byzantine Museum.

Immediately southeast of Tahtakale and Chrysaliniotissa is the massive tunnel-like **Famagusta Gate** **F** originally the main entrance to the medieval city. Restored during the early 1980s as the first of the local gentrification projects, it now operates as a cultural centre open only during events. The masoned barrel vaults provide an atmospheric setting for concerts, plays and art exhibitions.

Two blocks south of the Archbishop's Palace, at Patriarchou Grigoriou 20, the **House of Hadjigeorgakis Kornesios (Ethnological Museum)** G (22305316; charge) is a beautiful 1793 structure with a Gothic-style doorway and overhanging, enclosed balcony. The thoroughly renovated Ottoman-style interior is notable for its period furnishings, ornate stairway and grand reception room. It attests the wealth of Kornesios, the *dragoman* or official mediator between the Turkish sultan and Cypriot archbishop. The museum and mansion are undergoing renovations and are set to reopen in December 2025.

A short walk west along Patriarchou Grigoriou brings you to Plateia Tillyrias, dominated by the **Ömeriye Mosque** H, transformed from the Augustinian monastic church of St Mary's by the Ottoman conquerors. The mosque is still used for Muslim worship but is open to visitors outside of prayer times. The late sixteenth-century ***hamam*** or Turkish bath across the square has been meticulously restored, and functions as a contemporary spa with a full

Icon of Christ in Nicosia's Byzantine Museum and Art Galleries

Selimiye Mosque

range of treatments available (Hamam Omerye, www.hamamomerye.com).

Northern Nicosia

Compared with the bustling southern half of the city, northern Nicosia is quieter and poorer, though this is changing fast. The Ledra/Lokmacı pedestrian crossing point is conveniently close to a cluster of the most interesting sights in the North, making even the shortest visit worthwhile.

From much of the city, you will glimpse the minarets of the **Selimiye Camii** ❶ (Selimiye Mosque or Agiaa Sofia; open during prayer times; donation expected), which was formerly the Gothic Cathedral of the Holy Wisdom, begun in 1209 and consecrated in 1326 (though never actually completed). Here, Lusignan rulers were crowned kings of Cyprus; the Ottomans turned it into a mosque after the 1570 conquest, whitewashing over all the figural imagery but leaving soaring arches intact. After a long a period of restoration, it re-opened to visitors in the spring of 2025.

Next door, the **Bedesten** ❶ began life as a sixth-century Byzantine church before being enlarged as the Catholic church of St Nicholas of the English during the fourteenth century. Under the Ottomans it served briefly as a grain store and lockable cloth market before being abandoned. It re-emerged in 2009 following UN-sponsored (and EU- and Evkaf-funded) renovations, so you can once again admire the building's glory, including the magnificent north portal with its relief carving. Across the street is a functioning bazaar, the **Belediye Pazari** (Municipal Market), widely known as the Bandabulya. It was rebuilt for structural reasons, but at the cost of its former atmosphere – and the expulsion of most of the old stall-holders. Across Selimiye Meydanı, beyond the apse of the Selimiye Camii, stands the **Lapidary Museum** Ⓚ, (charge) a Lusignan building filled with intricately carved stonework of every description.

West of the mosque, Asma Altı Sokağı leads past a couple of old Turkish *hans* (courtyarded inns). The **Büyük Han** Ⓛ (Great Inn) is one of the oldest (1572) purpose-built Ottoman structures on the island. It has been thoroughly and tastefully restored, and is now home to small art galleries, workshops and a café-restaurant. The nearby **Kumarcılar Hanı** (Gamblers' Inn) hosts a café-restaurant and some small shops. Also nearby is the **Büyük Hamam** (Great Bath; www.nicosiagrandturkishbath.com), a converted Lusignan church, which, like its South Nicosia counterpart, has been thoughtfully overhauled. At the far end of Asma Alti Sokağı is Sarayönü Square, officially **Atatürk Square** Ⓜ, the hub of Turkish-Cypriot Nicosia. Its central granite column was probably brought from Salamis by the Venetians.

From the square, head north along Girne Caddesi to the **Mevlevî Tekke** Ⓝ. This was once a ceremonial hall used by the Mevlevî 'whirling dervish' sect, outlawed in Turkey in 1925 but surviving in Cyprus until 1954. The multi-domed, seventeenth-century building now has displays on the dervishes' daily life, including mannequins holding the musical instruments essential to the whirling ceremony. The building itself is

NOTES

The motorway network linking Nicosia and all the coastal resorts in South Cyprus makes for speedy transfers, but there's much to be said for pottering along on a slower route.

the star exhibit, but an arresting sight is the room packed with the tombs of 16 Mevlevî sheiks. Near here, the **Keryneia Gate** (Girne Kapısı) is northern Nicosia's only original Venetian gate, built in 1567, restored in 1821, but isolated since 1931 when the British cut great gaps in the walls to either side to permit passage of traffic to the rest of Northern Cyprus. It now houses a tourist office (392 227 29 94; www.visitncy.com)

Around South Nicosia

The following excursions all lie within 50km of southern Nicosia, making them easy day-trips.

Tamassos Archaeological Site (22622619; charge) ❷, an ancient city-kingdom dependent on copper mining, is just over 20km southwest of the capital, near the village of Politiko. Here excavations have uncovered a sanctuary and altar dedicated to Aphrodite/Astarte; although its importance is difficult to appreciate given its currently ruinous state, the discovery of copper traces in the temple demonstrated that metallurgy was sacred and that priests may have controlled the enterprise. Of more general interest are two royal tombs (sixth century BC). In each, stairways descend to a narrow *dromos* – a passage carved in stone to imitate wooden surfaces, complete with simulated bolted doors, windowsills and 'log-roof' ceilings. A set of magnificent stone lions and sphinxes which guarded the tombs are on display at the Cyprus Museum (see page 39).

From here a scenic, back-road drive leads to the monastery of **Machairas (Makherás)** ❸, (www.machairas.cy; free) 884m up in the rugged Pitsilia region. The monastery itself is a modern construction; an 1892 fire destroyed the original twelfth-century foundation, although an allegedly miracle-working icon of the Virgin survived, and modern frescoes are of a high standard.

The region (and the monastery itself) was a hideout for EOKA's second-in-command Grigoris Afxentiou, who was burnt alive at the conclusion of a protracted battle with the British near the monastery in 1957. The site of his death (a cave just below the monastery) is decorated with wreaths and is a place of pilgrimage for Greek Cypriots; inside the monastery a one-room museum documents the man and his grisly end.

Monastery of Machairas

Down the road beyond Lazanias and Gourri, the officially protected but rather lifeless village of **Fikardou (Fikárdhou)** represents a worthy effort to sustain Cypriot rural traditions, rating as a Unesco World Heritage Site. Its subtly coloured eighteenth- and nineteenth-century stone and mud-straw houses along cobbled streets have been restored with intent to revitalize the community. Alas, it does not seem to be working. In 1992, when the scheme was in its infancy, there were just eight permanent residents, and the population has remained at about the same number. Wend your way past the church to the museum-houses of **Katsinioros** and **Achilleas Dimitri** (22634 731; free), where you can see authentic old furnishings, a spinning wheel and loom, an olive press and a *zivanía* still.

Asinou Church

Stranded somewhat in the middle of nowhere just outside Nikitari, 50km west of Nicosia, is **Panagia Asinou** ❹, also known as Panagia Forviotissa, one of the gems of the Troödos foothills. From

Nicosia take the road beyond Peristerona, then follow the signs to the twelfth-century hillside church, famous for its magnificent Byzantine frescoes (also see page 69).

This modest but exquisite little stone-built, pitch-roofed church contains a veritable gallery of Byzantine art from the twelfth century, some skilfully overpainted 250 years later. A booklet explaining the different styles and subjects of the frescoes is usually available. Failing that, the highlights are a complete cycle of the life of Christ in the middle recess of the ceiling, and the apsidal frescoes of the Virgin flanked by archangels and Christ offering Communion to the apostles. If you find the church closed go back to the village of Nikitari and search out the local priest who looks after the key – either in the central café, or by phoning 99 830329.

Larnaka and the East

Highlights

- **The seafront**, see page 51
- **Agios Lazaros**, see page 52
- **Larnaka's Museums**, see page 52
- **West of Larnaka**, see page 53
- **Stavrovouni, Lefkara and Choirokoitia,** see page 54
- **East to Agia Napa**, see page 57
- **Cape Gkreko**, see page 58

Sprawling along the western shore of the wide bay that bears its name, **Larnaka (Larnaca)** ❺ retains a holiday resort atmosphere while at the same time hosting Cyprus' main international airport and the country's second-busiest port (after Limassol).

Much of northern Larnaka is built over the ancient city-kingdom of Kition. Legend attributes its founding to the Phoenician Kittim, a grandson of Noah, but Mycenaean dwellings discovered from the second millennium BC make this the oldest continuously inhabited city in Cyprus. The Phoenicians prospered here from the export of copper, and many centuries later Lusignan barons revived the town as a commercial and shipping centre. Under the Ottomans, foreign merchants and the consulates needed to protect their interests gave the town a cosmopolitan air.

The seafront

The palm-lined **Foinikoudes** (Finikoúdhes, 'Palm Trees') **Promenade** is home to hotels, chic cafés and fast-food eateries; at the north end is the pleasure-boat marina. A bust of the Athenian commander Kimon, who led a fleet to recapture Kition from the Persians in 450 BC (but died in the attempt), is a reminder of an ancient past.

From the marina, the compacted, dark-sand town beach stretches almost to the old fort that marks the edge of what was the Muslim quarter. **Larnaka Fort** (24304576; charge), originally Lusignan but adapted by the Ottomans, houses exhibits from its own history and serves as a venue for cultural events. From the ramparts, there are good views of the coastline. Opposite is the **Cami Kebir**, a converted Lusignan church still functioning as a place of worship for local Egyptians, Syrians and Iranians. Notice the tombstones topped with

Agios Lazaros, Larnaka

Turbanned tombstones in the Cami Kebir's graveyard

stone turbans in the graveyard, a rare sight so close to a mosque.

Agios Lazaros

Some 300m inland from here looms the three-tiered campanile of the town's most revered church, **Agios Lazaros** (www.agioslazaros.org), dedicated to the man the New Testament tells us Jesus raised from the dead. According to legend, the locals of Bethany, his hometown, were decidedly unimpressed by the miracle, expelling Lazarus in a not particularly seaworthy boat that nevertheless got him as far as Kition. Here, where he was more appreciated, Lazarus settled, became bishop and some thirty years later died (this time for good). The church erected over his tomb has been rebuilt many times, most recently in an extravagant mix of Byzantine, Romanesque and Gothic styles, and it has a fine iconostasis. The purported remains of Lazarus were taken from here to Constantinople in 898; in the crypt below the iconostasis you can see the empty but still venerated sarcophagus.

Larnaka's Museums

Opposite the marina, housed in refurbished former customs warehouses, are the **Larnaka Municipal Cultural Centre** (larnakaregion.com; free), whose art gallery has a changing programme of exhibits by local and foreign artists. Across from the nearby tourist office, on Zinonos Kitieos, is the town's best private collection, the **Pierides Marfin Laïki Bank Museum** (24145375; charge). Housed in an old family mansion are hundreds of archaeological finds and works of art from all over the island, tracing Cypriot culture from Chalcolithic to Lusignan times. Highlights include the famous 'Howling Man' of 3000 BC from Souskiou, painted Archaic and Attic pottery, cruciform picrolite idols, an antiquarian map gallery, Byzantine and Lusignan glazed ceramics, Roman glassware and Cypriot embroidery.

Larnaka District Archaeological Museum (24304169; charge) is a 10-minute walk northwest of the city centre beyond Leoforos (Avenue) Grigori Afxentiou, on Kimonos opposite the handsome Catholic convent of St Joseph. Of principal interest here are a reconstructed tomb from nearby Choirokoitia (see page 56), and Bronze Age pottery, in particular an amphora with a rampant octopus, and a *krater* (wine goblet) in the form of a fish.

West of Larnaka

About 3km southwest of the town, in the direction of the airport, lies the **Salt Lake** that provided a valuable source of income to ancient Larnaka. Lying 3m below sea level, it is a true lake only in winter and early spring. The salt was once collected annually at the end of July, after the lake dried up, but today pollution has rendered it unfit for human consumption. From November to February migratory flamingos gather here, although their numbers are declining.

The **Hala Sultan Tekke** ❻ (24643618; free), seems mirage-like in summer, thrusting its minaret through greenery and palm trees beyond the blinding salt flats. This shrine contains the remains of the Prophet Mohammed's wet nurse, Umm Haram ('Sacred Mother'), known as Hala Sultan in Turkish, and is Cyprus' most important place of Muslim pilgrimage. According to tradition, Umm Haram came to Cyprus with Arab invaders in 649. She fell from her mule near the Salt Lake, broke her neck and was

NOTES

The southeast corner of Cyprus is not only a major resort area, but the island's vegetable garden. Potatoes, aubergines, tomatoes, cucumbers and onions are all grown for export in the fertile red soil of the Kokkinochoria (Red Villages) district.

buried here. The present-day mosque around the tomb dates from 1816.

The outer room has brightly painted octagonal columns and a women's gallery to the right. In the inner sanctuary, the guardian (who also acts as a guide) will point out the trilithon structure above Umm Haram's grave: two enormous stones about 4.5m high, covered with a meteorite said to have come from Mt Sinai and to have hovered in the air here by itself for centuries.

Some 8km further is the village of Kiti and its church of **Panagia Angeloktisti** ❼ (Our Lady 'Built by Angels'; 4424646; photography allowed without flash). Constructed in honey-toned stone, the domed eleventh-century edifice replaces a much earlier structure. Its outstanding feature is a splendid fifth- or sixth-century Byzantine **mosaic** in the apse, among the finest works of Byzantine art in Cyprus. A standing Virgin holds the Christ Child, flanked by the archangels Michael and Gabriel.

Stavrovouni, Lefkara and Choirokoitia

The famous mountaintop monastery of **Stavrovouni** ❽ (Mountain of the Cross; 22533630; free; men only) is located just off the A1 Limassol–Nicosia motorway. At an altitude of 750m, it has superb views north to Nicosia and the hazy Pentadaktylos Mountains, and south to the Salt Lake, Larnaka and the sea.

Stavrovouni was built on the site of a shrine to Aphrodite, which, like the monastery today, was off-limits to women. Nevertheless, Helena, mother of Emperor Constantine, is said to have ventured up here in AD 327 to found the monastery and endow it with a piece of the True Cross. The relic is still proudly displayed in the monastery church. Note that cameras or videos are forbidden anywhere in the grounds. It is really not a place for casual tourism, and there is nothing extraordinary to see other than the view; the handful of monks follow the strictest regimen on the island, based on that of Mt Athos in Greece.

At the foot of the winding road up to Stavrovouni is **Agia Varvara** (Ayía Varvára) monastery (men only). Most of the local monks live here, as conditions up on the exposed summit are harsh, with only a half-dozen brothers resident there at any one time. Adjacent was formerly the studio of Brother Kallinikos (1920–2011), regarded (controversially in some quarters) as one of the best icon painters of his age.

Lefkara ❾, 40km west of Larnaka, is actually two villages – Pano Lefkara and Kato Lefkara – nestled in the foothills of the Troödos Mountains. Lefkara is synonymous with *lefkarítika*, the traditional embroidery that has brought the village fame for more than five centuries. Widely but incorrectly termed 'lacework', *lefkarítika* is actually linen openwork, stitched with intricate geometric patterns. Furthermore, quite a lot of what's peddled here is imported and machine-produced – beware. The village is equally

Church at the mountaintop monastery of Stavrovouni

renowned for its silver-smithing, and hallmarked silver jewellery may be a more reliable and better-value purchase.

Some women still work in the narrow streets and courtyards of Pano (Upper) Lefkara, patiently turning out embroidered articles which you can buy from them or in one of the many shops. There are more sales outlets than strictly necessary, and as a result hustling, albeit of a mild kind, is common practice.

Smaller and mostly overlooked is Kato (Lower) Lefkara, an attractive village, with many of its traditional houses recently restored and window and door frames painted in bright Mediterranean blue. In a field to one side stands the twelfth-century church of **Archangelos** (always open), with damaged but still intriguing frescoes dating from the twelfth to fifteenth centuries.

Archaeologically inclined visitors should head south to Choirokoitia (Khirokitiá), the modern village adjacent to the **Choirokoitia Neolithic Settlement** ⑩ (24322710; charge). Among the oldest sites in Cyprus, it dates to just after 7000 BC. The most interesting of the four areas is the main street, with its foundations of beehive-shaped houses called *tholoi*. Artefacts discovered here are on show at Nicosia's Cyprus Museum (see page 39).

NOTES

An intriguing boat trip from Agia Napa goes as far as the marine border at Famagusta to view the decaying town of Varosha. Once a major resort, it has been left to rot since 1974, when it was declared UN territory (though it is policed by the Turkish army). Since 2020, a section of Varosha's abandonded town is open to the public, though heavily militarized. Untouched since the invasion, a visit offers a harrowing glimpse of the past and remnants of pre-war Cyprus.

East to Agia Napa

Just beyond the resort hotels northeast of Larnaka, both A3 motorway and surface roads pass through the

Agia Napa's famous beaches

Dhekelia British Sovereign Base Area. You emerge back into Greek-Cypriot territory on the east at Xylofagou. Seaward of this is **Potamos Liopetriou** ⓫, a picturesque inlet jammed with small, gaily painted fishing boats, flanked by a couple of popular seafood tavernas. At the time of writing, there were ongoing roadworks refurbishing the area. Plans include the construction of a bridge connecting the east and west banks of the river, platforms for amateur and professional fishermen, walking trails and bike paths. It is still possible to visit the fish tavernas.

Following the Turkish occupation of Famagusta, **Agia Napa** ⓬ (Ayía Nápa) was transformed from a tiny fishing village into Cyprus' major resort. Indeed, it has developed a reputation as one of the Mediterranean's most notorious clubbing destinations. The change is most pronounced in the square around the **monastery of Agia Napa** (Our Lady of the Forest; undergoing renovations at the time of writing and closed to visitors). The only forest here, really, is furnished by two six hundred-year-old giant sycamore figs in the monastery grounds.

However, during the day (when the clubbers are asleep or at the beach), the town centre is often peaceful. The monastery, built around 1500, remains one of Cyprus' most handsome Venetian buildings, with an octagonal marble fountain in the Gothic cloister.

It is now a conference centre for the World Council of Churches, and its church is open regularly for Sunday services.

Agia Napa's growth is largely a result of its fine **beaches** of golden sand. The most famous one, 2km west of the centre, is **Nissi**, a picture-postcard strip and cove with limpid blue waters and a tiny island within paddling distance. At nearby **Makronisos**, another popular beach, there are nineteen rock tombs dating from the classical and Hellenistic periods. East of the little port stretches **Kryo Nero**, less scenic but equally sandy.

Cape Gkreko

The coast road east towards **Cape Gkreko** ⓭, the island's south-eastern tip, offers spectacular rocky inlets, caves and bays providing an escape from the crowds.

Just outside Agia Napa, beside the Grecian Bay Hotel, the **Thalassines Spilies** (Sea Caves) are famous for a much-photographed sea arch and frequented by snorkellers and divers. A few kilometres further along the main road yawn the more spectacular **Spilies sta Palatia** (Palace Caves).

Further still is the **Cape Gkreko viewpoint**. You have to walk the last 500m uphill, but it is well worth the effort. From an altitude of almost 100m, the clifftop view looking west is stupendous. Just to the east is Cape Gkreko itself. The point is occupied by military installations and radio transmitters, so is off-limits.

Heading north will bring you to **Konnos Bay**, one of the most picturesque sandy coves in Cyprus, with a watersports franchise. On a quiet day, it can be heaven, though always very shallow. In midsummer, Agia Napa 'booze cruises' and their sound systems disturb the peace. Due to concerns about the bay being a fire hazard, parking is now prohibited along the narrow forest track leading to Konnos Beach; use the new car park outside the wooded area instead.

The coast road continues north to the purpose-built resort of **Protaras**, with blue-flag beaches like Fig Tree Bay.

Limassol and the South Coast

Highlights

- **East of Limassol**, see page 61
- **West of Limassol**, see page 62
- **Kourion**, see page 63
- **West to Petra tou Romiou**, see page 65

Limassol ⓮ (*Lemesos* in Greek) is Cyprus' good-time town, with many restaurants, international companies and lively nightlife venues. Fittingly, the city hosts the island's most exuberant pre-Lenten Carnival. In addition, it boasts Cyprus' busiest harbour, a luxurious Marina and was formerly the focal point of much of the wine industry. Most accommodation is away from the centre in a strip of high-rise shoreline hotels extending 16km east.

Crusading English king Richard the Lionheart stopped off at Limassol in 1191, deposed the tyrannical Byzantine usurper Isaac Komnenos and then proceeded to sell Cyprus – first to the Knights Templar, subsequently to the Lusignans. The crusader Knights of St John made the environs of Limassol their headquarters in 1291, after which the town flourished for some centuries.

Konnos Bay

Cami Kebir minaret in Limassol

By the early nineteenth century, earthquakes and medieval raids by the Mamelukes and Genoese had reduced the city to an insignificant village. British development of the wine industry breathed new life into it and, since the 1974 partition, greater Limassol's population has almost doubled to 185,000, second only to that of Nicosia.

The only surviving medieval monument is **Limassol Castle** Ⓐ, an imposing, thirteenth- to fourteenth-century stone fortification near the old port. Today it houses the **Cyprus Medieval Museum** (25305419; charge), the island's best collection from these periods, with some well-preserved tombstones, bronze or brass tableware, and silver plates from the Lambousa Treasure showing events from the life of King David. The building itself, with its echoing vaults, air shafts and stairways, is equally interesting and has fine views from the battlements.

The area around the castle is particularly pleasant, with lush gardens and historic buildings. Immediately south and west lies the **Lanitis Carob Mill** restoration project, (carobmill-restaurants.com) with a selection of restaurants and bistros, an exhibition space, plus a small free display on the carob milling industry. The narrow lanes on all sides used to be the Turkish-Cypriot commercial quarter. The **Cami Kebir** (Great Mosque) Ⓑ, a few metres east, is still in use; there's a working Turkish bath (*hamam*) nearby. Also in this interesting quarter, you will find artisans' workshops where the speciality is copper and tinware, plus a selection of art and ceramics galleries.

Towards the coast, **Limassol Marina** (www.limassolmarina.com) is a hub of high-end boutique shops and restaurants where luxurious private yachts park. You can admire the seafront villas that exude wealth and are in contrast to the rest of the island. A stroll around here is worth it and there are a few affordable bars and restaurants, as well as the nearby Paradox Museum.

From the castle, it's a 10-minute walk along part-pedestrianized Agiou Andreou to the **Municipal Folk Art Museum** **C** (25362303; charge). It provides a glimpse of rural Cypriot life through wood-carving, embroidery, jewellery and weaving; and while it does have over five hundred exhibits, lighting and labelling are poor, and you must buy the guide booklet to get anything much out of the displays.

Further east, abutting the seafront promenade, are the **Municipal Gardens**, a pleasant place to rest for a while – take the kids, there is a playground area – and the venue for the annual late-summer wine festival. At the far end of the gardens, the small **Lemesos District Archaeological Museum** **D** (25 305157; charge) is – as so often in Cyprus – strongest on Archaic, Geometric and Bronze Age artefacts, in particular a *rhyton* in the form of a bull and small fertility idols with upraised arms, clasping their breasts or holding sacred mirrors of Aphrodite/Astarte.

East of Limassol

Some 11km east of the town, between two clusters of beach hotels, are the ruins of ancient **Amathus** **E** (25635226; charge), one of the island's oldest city-kingdoms. The ruins, dating back to 1100 BC, are centred on its *agora* (marketplace), and there is still quite a lot of it intact, with basilicas, a temple of Aphrodite and an elaborate waterworks system.

About 16km further on by motorway or surface road is **Governor's Beach** (Akti Kyvernitou) ⓯, actually several coves of dark sand contrasting sharply with white-chalk cliffs just behind. There are a few tavernas and clusters of low-rise accommodation right behind. Farther east along the coast, you reach **Zygi** ⓰, a former carob pod-loading port with a small marina and a cluster of seafood restaurants popular with Cypriots – though almost all the fare on offer is frozen or imported so ask for the fresh fish of the day.

West of Limassol

Traces of one of the earliest phases of human presence on the island – hunters of pygmy hippos from 9000 BC – were found on the **Akrotiri Peninsula** west of Limassol. Nearly half of the peninsula is made up of salt marsh, frequented by migratory birds, notably pink flamingos, from October to March. On the east coast of the peninsula is hard-packed **Lady's Mile Beach**, popular with Limassolians. Most of the peninsula is occupied by the airfield and other installations of the British Akrotiri Sovereign Base Area.

Ruins of ancient Amathus

Just north of the peninsula, the impressive fifteenth-century **Kolossi Castle** ⓱ (25934907;

charge) is one of the icons of Cypriot tourism. Once the headquarters of the Knights of St John, this is the base from where they administered their considerable sugar plantations and vineyards. The three-storey Commanderie, as the headquarters was known, gave its name to their prized Commandaria dessert wine, still produced today by commercial wineries.

Kourion

Before exploring the great archaeological site of Kourion, stop in nearby Episkopi village to do a little homework at the **Kourion Archaeological Museum** (25932453; free), which holds dramatic finds from the earthquake that devastated Kourion in AD 365. On display is a touching group of three human skeletons: archaeologists believe them to be of a 25-year-old male protecting a 19-year-old female with an 18-month-old baby clutched to her breast. Other exhibits include a Roman stone lion fountain, terracotta vases and figurines.

Just west of Episkopi is **Kourion** ⓲ itself (25934250; charge). Along with Salamis in the north (see page 87), this is the island's most important archaeological site, spectacularly set on a bluff above Episkopi Bay. Today, there's a broad, popular beach with a few shack-like tavernas at the base of the palisade.

Experts attribute the foundation of the town to Mycenaean settlers during the thirteenth century BC. Known as Curium to the Romans, it converted to Christianity in the fourth century; after the Arab raids of the seventh century, the bishopric moved to Episkopi, leaving Kourion to sink into oblivion.

Your first stop should be the reconstructed **Roman theatre** (AD 50–175), spectacularly perched on the edge of the bluff. The theatre once seated 3,500 and is now used for early-summer performances of Shakespeare plays, and concerts. Behind the theatre is the fourth-century AD **Annexe of Eustolios**. The floor mosaics of birds and fish indicate that Eustolios was a man of wealth and taste; a long inscription to Christ suggests that he was also a Christian convert. Eustolios later added an adjacent bathhouse, which he opened to destitute survivors of the earthquake, as attested by another inscription. Its central room features some more remarkable mosaics, including one of Ktisis, the female spirit of creation, wielding a Roman foot-ruler.

The extensive ruins of the city centre, 300m northwest along a graded path, include the *agora* (marketplace) with its *nymphaeum* (fountain house). Turn to the left to explore the remains of an early Christian **basilica**. The basilica's plan reveals twelve pairs of granite columns, recycled ancient masonry, for the nave. To the north is the **baptistry**, where new converts disrobed and were anointed with oil before descending to the cross-shaped font.

On the other side of the walkway is the **House of the Gladiators**, so named for its mosaics of two duels, one with an aristocratic-looking referee – perhaps the owner of the house. Nearby, also under a protective canopy, is the **Achilles mosaic**. It depicts Achilles, disguised as a woman to avoid enlistment in the expedition to Troy, being tricked by Odysseus into grabbing a spear and shield and revealing his identity.

The **Sanctuary of Apollo Hylates/Ylatis** ⓳ (25934250; charge) lies 3km to the west. Apollo was worshipped here as god of the woodlands as early as the eighth century BC, but most of the present structures were put up around AD 100 and destroyed in the earthquake of 365.

From the ticket booth, take the path west to the pilgrims' entrance (through the remains of the Pafos Gate). The buildings here

NOTES

Petra tou Romiou has long inspired legends, as before Digenis Akritas' time it was reputed to be the birthplace of Aphrodite, who emerged from the sea here (though Kythera Island in Greece also strenuously claims this honour).

were probably hostels and storehouses for worshippers' votive offerings. The surplus was carefully placed in the *vothros* pit (at the centre of the site), which was full of terracotta figurines, mostly horse riders – still intact when uncovered by the archaeologists. Follow the sanctuary's main street to the **Temple of Apollo**, which has been partially reconstructed to look as it did in AD 100.

House of the Gladiators, Kourion

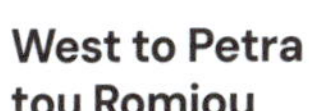

West to Petra tou Romiou

If the flat, hard-packed sands of Kourion Beach don't appeal to you, try the looser, coarse sand-and-shingle of **Avdimou** (Evdhímou) Beach, about 10km further west, with two tavernas. But if you crave the creature comforts of a resort, then continue on to **Pissouri** ⓴. The latter is an attractive, sheltered place, with a coarse but fairly long sand-and-shingle beach, plus ample accommodation and eating opportunities just behind.

West of Pissouri, just beyond the border into Pafos district, a huge sea-washed monolith juxtaposed with white cliffs behind is the famous **Petra tou Romiou** ㉑. This is named for legendary Byzantine hero Digenis Akritas, aka Romios, who used the big rock (*pétra* in Greek) plus smaller ones around it as missiles against Arab seaborne raiders. Opposite the rocks, along the B6 road, a parking area gets very crowded at sunset. The beach here is mostly coarse gravel, and the water is often storm-stirred.

Troödos Mountains

Highlights

- **Platres to Troödos**, see page 66
- **Kakopetria and Galata**, see page 68
- **Marathassa**, see page 70
- **West to Kykkou**, see page 71
- **Eastern Troödos churches**, see page 72

The **Troödos (Troödhos) Mountains** in central Cyprus are the island's principal upland – and pronounced, approximately, 'troh-dhos' rather than 'true-dos' as many foreigners are apt to say. They provide many things: a breath of fresh air for hot and flustered visitors and locals, a splendid collection of tiny Byzantine churches scattered around the hillsides, wonderful walking trails and, most importantly, much of the island's fresh water.

Roads up the mountain climb through foothills with rushing streams and orchards, past villages perched on the slopes, surrounded at higher altitudes by pine forest. Historically, monks and Greek-Cypriot EOKA fighters found refuge here; more recently the monasteries have been joined by resort hotels, with even a little winter skiing near the resort of Troödos. On the southern slopes in Limassol district, up to the 1,000m-high contour, are the vineyards and villages that produce most of Cyprus' wine.

Platres to Troödos

At an altitude of 1,200m, **Pano Platres** ㉒ makes a good base for visiting the entire Troödos region. This little 'hill station' occupies a charming and shady mountain site and comprises several hotels, large numbers of private villas, restaurants and shops. The main pastime here is walking, and the Ministry of Tourism has marked several nearby mountain trails, aimed at most ability levels – get details at the Platres tourist office. It's worth noting that the Cyprus

Tourism Organization (CTO or KOT in Greek) was renamed Visit Cyprus but many signs still refer to it by its former name. The most popular hike is the 2km trail up to the pretty **Kaledonia Falls**. The walk starts at the Psilodendhro restaurant and trout farm just outside Platres, and is well marked.

Omodos (Ómodhos) ㉓, renovated as a showpiece wine-producing village, lies 8km southwest of Platres. It's an attractive place, but has become over-commercialized, and the tour buses diminish the atmosphere their occupants have come to savour. However, you can still find calm in the village's monastery of **Timios Stavros** (True Cross), which dominates the broad, cobbled square in front of it – probably an example of Lusignan urban planning.

All roads in the mountains seem to lead to the eponymous resort of **Troödos** ㉔, which at 1,676m is the island's highest facility. There are ski slopes nearby, while in spring and autumn it's a good starting point for dedicated ramblers. Avoid midsummer, when its single main street turns into an overcrowded promenade of kitsch stalls and rumbling tour buses. A short drive away from Troödos square, in an old Asbestos mine is the Troodos Geopark Visitor Centre (25420145; www.troodosgeopark.com) which helps orientate visitors to

Typical village in the Troödos Mountains

Old quarter of Kakopetria

the high mountains, and provides maps and information on the local wildlife and plants.

Mt Olympos (1,952m), Cyprus' tallest peak, also known locally as Chionistra (Khionístra, 'Snow-Tipped'), is best visited by car up a narrow road. For security reasons, you have to walk the final distance up to the giant British radar 'golf ball' and Cypriot installations on the double-humped summit, and the views are surprisingly limited. It's preferable to tackle one of two nature trails – the Atalante or the Artemis – that circle the peak.

Kakopetria and Galata

Kakopetria ㉕, chief village of the Solea region north of the Troödos ridgeline, is easily reached by fast roads from Nicosia, and is accordingly popular at weekends and holidays. The highlight of the place is its ridgeline **old quarter**, a protected ensemble that's now home to recommendable eating and accommodation. This historic part of town is essentially one long, narrow street running parallel to the leafy river. The string of houses, with their river-view balconies, have been restored to bring out the subtle russet, amber and silver hues of the local stone.

Just outside the village is one of the Troödos Mountains' most famous frescoed churches, **Agios Nikolaos tis Stegis** (St Nicholas of the Roof; 22922583). The name refers to the upper roof of shingles, built in the fifteenth century to shelter the older domed roof of tiles. Inside, the oldest frescoes date from the church's foundation in the eleventh century, but the most unusual ones – including the Virgin nursing the infant Jesus, and the Angel at the Tomb – are from some centuries later.

Just north of Kakopetria, **Galata** ㉖ has another Unesco-listed church of 1502, **Panagia tis Podithou**; the key-holder can be contacted at the café in the village square (99348735). Although its

FRESCOED CHURCHES

The Troödos Mountains' remarkable painted churches were built between the eleventh and sixteenth centuries. For visitors, their astonishing degree of preservation and the beauty of their artwork makes for compulsive viewing. For scholars, the churches provide a fascinating lesson in provincial Byzantine and post-Byzantine art; there is nothing else like them in the Mediterranean other than the country churches of Crete and Rhodes. The original function of the frescoes was as religious cartoon strips, teaching the simple, illiterate and often isolated parishioners the lessons of the Gospels; today they serve as a fascinating document of Lusignan and Venetian life, as the painters – mostly anonymous – interpreted Biblical episodes with contemporary medieval personalities and dress. Most of the churches have been listed on Unesco's World Cultural Heritage register.

The densest concentration of painted churches lies on the north slopes Troödos, where Panagia Asinou (see page 49), Agios Nikolaos tis Stegis (in Kakopetria), Panagia tis Podithou (in Galata), Agios Ioannis Lambadistis (in Kalopanagiotis) and Panagia tou Araka (near Lagoudera) are all within a short drive of each other. Some have set visiting hours; for others you will have to contact the key-holder, either a priest or lay person, who lives nearby. Mobile phone numbers are usually posted on the church door, otherwise ask at the local coffee shop. Photography, certainly with flash or tripod, is rarely if ever allowed.

Panagia tou Araka, one of the painted church in the Troödos Mountains

very Italianate fresco decoration was never completed, what does exist – including an extravagantly secular Crucifixion over the west door, Solomon and David flanking the Communion of the Apostles in the apse – justifies the trouble of gaining admission. The same key-keeper will then escort you to **Archangelos** (aka Panagia Theotokou) nearby, dating from 1514 and containing an unusually complete cycle portraying the life of Christ.

Marathassa

Easily reached either from Troödos resort or from Kakopetria, the **Marathassa** valley west of Solea is home to more mountain villages and painted churches. From either start point, the first village reached is **Pedoulas** ㉗, famous for its cherries – and its church of **Archangelos Michail**, built in 1474. Vivid frescoes, cleaned during the 1980s, include The Sacrifice of Abraham, and a Baptism complete with fish in the River Jordan. In **Moutoullas** village, 3km downhill, you'll find the earliest of the frescoed churches, **Panagia tou Moutoulla**, built in about 1280 (22 952 677 or 97 733 480 to arrange a visit). The frescoes, while not the most expressive hereabouts, are unretouched and idiosyncratic. If time is short, prioritize attractive **Kalopanagiotis** ㉘ (Kalopanayiótis) village, 1km further along, whose star is the intact riverside monastery of **Agios Ioannis Lambadistis** (22 952

580). The main church is actually triple, with different fresco cycles completed at various times between the thirteenth and fifteenth centuries; most of them have been carefully restored since 2009 by students of London's Courtauld Institute of Art. The northernmost, Latin chapel, with the most complete Italo-Byzantine sequence on the island, was clearly painted by a local artist who had spent extensive time in Italy. In one wing of the monastery buildings is a rewarding gallery of Byzantine and post-Byzantine icons.

West to Kykkou

The main roads west from either Pedoulas or Kalopanagiotis lead quickly to the gem that is the monastery of **Panagia tis Kykkou** ㉙ (pronounced Tchýkou in dialect; kykkos.org.cy), proudly remote from the world on a mountainside surrounded by pine forest.

Kykkou is the richest and most important monastery on the island. Founded in 1094 by a hermit, it grew in prestige when Emperor Alexis Komnenos (ruled 1081–1118) gave it a rich land grant and an icon of the Virgin supposedly painted by St Luke, but now covered in gilded silver. Its legendary rain-making powers still bring in farmers to pray in times of drought.

But apart from the precious icon and a few other pieces, there is little of historical value here, since the monastery was gutted by fire four times between 1365 and 1813. Frankly garish mosaics and frescoes lining every vertical surface are workmanlike at best. Kykkou is primarily a place of pilgrimage and a preferred venue for baptisms, when proud relatives cheerfully ignore the ban on photography and videoing enforced against the heterodox, who can occasionally be met with faint hostility. In the quieter museum you can learn about Kykkou's history and see some of its finest treasures.

Kykkou is also famous for having had Archbishop Makarios among its novices (he is buried on a hill above the monastery). During the 1950s, Kykkou served as a communications and supply

Catch of the day, Pafos harbour

base for EOKA, and thus became a symbol of the Cypriot nationalist struggle.

West of Kykkou, onward roads lead downhill into the **Cedar Valley** (Koilada tou Kedron) ㉚, one of the signal successes of the island's reforestation programme. This steep-sided ravine hosts thousands of indigenous cedar trees (*Cedrus brevifolia*), first cousins to the more famous cedars of Lebanon. Nearby, around Tripylos peak, is a small reserve dedicated to the protection of the indigenous, formerly endangered Cypriot wild mountain sheep, the moufflon.

Eastern Troödos churches

If you've developed a taste for frescoed churches, there are several more in the eastern half of the Troödos, easily accessible from Platres or Kakopetria. The most spectacular of these, just north of **Lagoudera** ㉛ (Lagoudherá) village, is **Panagia tou Araka** (Our Lady of the Wild Vetch; 99557369), with most frescoes dating from 1192. The more unusual include a fine dome Pandokrator (Christ in Majesty), the only one in the Troödos, and adjacent, finely observed Presentations of Christ and the Virgin near the apse.

In **Pelendri** (Peléndhri) ㉜, fourteenth-century **Stavros** at the village outskirts (99909393/99662286) features scenes from the life of the Virgin. Much closer to Limassol, **Louvaras** village ㉝ can offer deceptively tiny **Agios Mamas** church, crammed full of well-preserved frescoes from 1495 by Philip Goul, one of the few identified local painters.

Off the eastern edge of the Troödos, at **Palaichori** ❸❹, you'll find another member of the roster of UNESCO mountain churches, **Metamorfosis tou Sotiros** (Transfiguration of the Saviour; 22643012), dating from the fifteenth and sixteenth centuries and containing (predictably) a fine representation of the Transfiguration.

Pafos and the West

Highlights

- **Kato Pafos**, see page 74
- **Kato Pafos to Ktima**, see page 75
- **Ktima**, see page 76
- **Southeast of Pafos**, see page 77
- **North of Pafos**, see page 79

Once a sleepy fishing port, **Pafos** (Páphos) ❸❺ has been transformed into a booming resort town. But visitors who want more than just sun and sand have plenty to occupy them. Ancient Nea Paphos was Cyprus' Roman capital and has a wealth of historic sites. It is also a good base for exploring nearby hill-villages and the rugged Akamas Peninsula.

Legend attributes the founding of nearby Palaia (Old) Paphos to the priest-king Kinyras, and that city-kingdom gained renown as the centre of Aphrodite's cult. The last king of Palaia Paphos, Nikokles, established the port of Nea (New) Paphos during the fourth century BC, though Palaia Paphos remained the centre of Aphrodite worship until the fourth century AD. Within one hundred years of its founding, Nea Paphos surpassed Salamis as the chief city of Cyprus. However, earthquakes in 332 and 342 and the Arab attacks of the seventh century forced most of the population inland to Ktima. Medieval Pafos languished as a miserable, unsanitary seaport; however, under the British the population gradually rose from about 2,000 to about 9,000 in 1960. It continued to grow and prosper, with the opening of Pafos International Airport in 1985 firmly establishing it as a resort, and later as a major second- (or first-) home venue for foreigners.

Kato Pafos

Heavily developed Kato (Lower) Pafos, along the seaside, is where most visitors stay. The harbour still provides a picturesque haven for fishing and excursion boats as it curves around a jetty to the **Medieval Fort** Ⓐ (26306217; charge), all that remains of a much larger Lusignan castle. The Ottomans used it as a prison, the British as a salt warehouse; it is currently empty, with only the rooftop views justifying the admission fee. In the summer, festivals are held in front of the castle.

With the harbour on your left, walk towards the large, modern shed-like building in the distance. Beyond this lie the famous **Paphos Mosaics** Ⓑ (www.visitpafos.org.cy). These splendid decorative floors were uncovered in the remains of luxurious Roman villas of the second to the fifth centuries AD. The 'houses' are named after the mosaics'

Ancient ruins in Pafos

most prominent motifs. The **House of Dionysos** displays the god of wine riding a chariot drawn by two panthers, flanked by satyrs and slaves. This and other scenes, such as Dionysos offering a bunch of grapes to the nymph Akme, and Ikarios of Athens getting shepherds drunk with their first taste of wine, were customary decorations for banqueting halls. The **House of Aion** has a spectacular five-panelled mosaic, whose central panel depicts Aion, god of eternity, judging a beauty contest between a smug-looking Queen Cassiopeia (the winner) and unhappy, prettier water nymphs departing on assorted sea-monsters. The single other villa open to the public, the **House of Theseus**, features the first bath of the infant Achilles.

A short walk north leads to the restored **Odeion** Ⓒ, a small theatre dating from the second century AD, built entirely of hewn limestone blocks. In a picturesque hillside setting, it seats 1,250 spectators for musical and theatrical performances held occasionally in the summer. Excavations by a team from the Jagiellonian University of Krakow on the adjacent **agora**, which started in 1965, revealed that it was the central square court of the city.

Kato Pafos to Ktima

From the harbourside car parks and public bus terminal, first Apostolou Pavlou, and then Stassandrou, climb towards the remains of fourth-century AD **Agia Kyriaki** basilica Ⓓ. Amid the ruins of the seven-aisled church, you can make out mosaic pavements with floral and geometric patterns and columns of green-and-white marble imported from Greece. Arabic graffiti on the columns dates from the invasion that destroyed the basilica in 653. One of the columns is called **St Paul's Pillar**, to which the apostle was (apocryphally) tied and lashed 39 times for preaching the Gospel. Amid the ruins is handsome post-Byzantine **Panagia Chrysopolitissa** church, sometimes also referred to as Agia Kyriaki (stpauls-catholic-parish-paphos.com).

A little further along Apostolou Pavlou is the intriguing sight of a tree festooned with hundreds of handkerchiefs and rags. It marks the **Catacomb of Agia Solomoni**, once regarded as a spot where prayers could be miraculously answered, and still doing a good trade with believers today. The tradition of tying a handkerchief or rag as a votive offering to a tree or bush at a sacred site is common in the Middle East. Just north of here, hacked out of the living rock on Fabrica hill, is the Australian-excavated **Hellenistic theatre** Ⓔ, one of the largest on Cyprus.

Still further northwest is ancient Nea Paphos' necropolis, the so-called **Tombs of the Kings** Ⓕ (26306295). The title is a misnomer, as the subterranean burial chambers hacked out of the soft rock here between the third century BC and the third century AD were meant for the local privileged class, not kings. The tomb architecture is based on Ptolemaic adaptations of Macedonian prototypes: spacious courtyards with Doric columns and decorative entablatures. Of the eight tomb complexes, numbers three, four and eight are the best.

Ktima

Set on a blufftop above the resort, the upper part of Pafos, known as **Ktima**, is a normal Cypriot provincial town compared to the coastal strip. After shopping at the colourful daily produce market and a variety of souvenir stalls, you can sit down for a drink or a meal in the narrow lanes of the old centre.

There are two small museums in the centre of Ktima. The **Ethnographical Museum of Pafos** Ⓖ (local English spelling; also known as the Eliades Collection; Exo Vrysis 1; www.ethnographicalmuseum.com; charge), opened in 1958, occupies a charming nineteenth-century house. It combines priceless antiques, a mocked-up rural room, basketry, old wagons and – in the garden – a genuine, third-century BC rock tomb. Nearby are the Municipal Gardens offering a small patch of green in the city. Find marble water fountains, statues and the neo-classical building of the Pafos Town Hall here.

The **Archaeological Museum of the Pafos District** Ⓗ (26 955 801) down the roadhouses some remarkable sculptures found in the House of Theseus (see page 75), including a statue of Asklepios (the Greek master of medicine) feeding an egg to the snake coiled around his staff. Also, look out for the Hellenistic clay hot-water bottles, specially moulded to fit all parts of the body. The completely restored and upgraded museum has some new finds from recent excavation works on display.

House of Theseus, Pafos

Southeast of Pafos

Just southeast of Pafos is the village of **Geroskipou** (Yeroskípou) ㊱, whose name derives from **Hieros Kipos**, meaning 'Sacred Garden'; pilgrims would stop here on their way to Aphrodite's temple at Palaia Paphos. The ninth-century church of **Agia Paraskevi** (26 961 859) in the centre of Geroskipou is a rare island example of a six-domed basilica. Inside are fine, if damaged, fifteenth-century murals and a much-revered icon from the same period, with a *Virgin and Child* on one side and a *Crucifixion* on the reverse.

In a restored house nearby is a **Folk Art Museum** (26 306 216; charge). Typical of a rich Cypriot's dwelling in the late eighteenth or early nineteenth century, the upper storey is ringed with handsome wooden balconies. Display rooms are thematic, devoted to crafts such as carding and ginning cotton, spinning and weaving, tinning vessels, and a reproduced cobbler's workshop.

From here, continue southeast along the B6 for about 12km to **Kouklia** 37, once Palaia Paphos (Palaipaphos), where the cult of Aphrodite was celebrated. The rites of the love goddess flourished at the **Sanctuary of Aphrodite** (26 432 155; charge). Most of the valuable finds have been taken to Nicosia, though after much bureaucratic wrangling the original of the famous second- or third-century AD mosaic of *Leda and the Swan* has been returned. It has pride of place in the **Palaipaphos Museum** (same as the Sanctuary; same ticket), inside the sturdy Château de Covocle (originally a Lusignan manor-farm). The museum galleries are upstairs from a thirteenth-century vaulted banquet hall, the acoustically superb venue for early summer chamber music concerts. Those with their own transport may want to continue inland to the so-called **Palaia Enkleistra** (key and instructions from museum staff in exchange for piece of ID), a fifteenth-century cave-hermitage with damaged but unique frescoes; on the ceiling, dating from the era when the Western and Orthodox churches were briefly united, is a rare depiction of the Holy Trinity.

Remains of fluted columns at the Sanctuary of Aphrodite

A WILDERNESS UNDER THREAT

Untamed and scenic, the last major piece of unspoilt coastline in South Cyprus, the Akamas Peninsula arouses strong passions among conservationists, hikers and wildlife-spotters on the one hand, and tourist-enterprise developers, the Orthodox Church and local villagers on the other. Since 1986, organizations as disparate as the World Bank, the European Union, Friends of the Earth and Greenpeace have called for the creation of a local national park. Matters are complicated by the entire peninsula being a patchwork of private land (Greek- and Turkish-Cypriot owned), state forest, village commons and church holdings. Landowners and residents have long argued it is unfair that they are not allowed to develop what has become prime real estate, and conservationists have volleyed back concerns over the threat of impinging development to one of Cyprus' last-remaining nature spots. In 2016, the government finally designated all state-owned land in Akamas as a national forest park. However, ongoing clashes between environmentalists and locals continue as the powers-that-be prepare for 'sustainable' development on government-owned land. Plans include building roads, control entry points, cafés, shops and other facilities in forests and on beaches, including the protected turtle-nesting site of Lara Bay. A backlash ensued from the Green Party who feel this would be just the start of spiralling development. Landowners too are angry, but at the government pocketing cash from tourist sites that they themselves have been denied from building. Finally, conservationists are concerned local authorities will try to appease private landowners with permits to build farms that welcome visitors on EU-protected Natura 2000 areas, which could easily be transformed into small hotels.

North of Pafos

Beaches in Pafos are unremarkable, so many visitors travel 10km north to better sands at **Coral Bay** (Kolpos Koralion). Further up the coast, there are more beaches either side of **Agios Georgios (Áyios**

The unspoiled Akamas Peninsula

Yeóryios), which has accommodation, restaurants and the remains of a basilica with mosaic flooring. Beyond pebbly 'White River Beach' just north of Agios Georgios, you'll pass sandier **Toxeftra** beach, and the turning inland to the famous **Avakas Gorge**, a favourite destination for hikers, with plenty of wildlife-spotting opportunities. Beyond here, it's best to have a 4WD vehicle as you head up to Lara Bay and the vast sandy beaches on either side. The northerly, dune-clad **Lara Bay** 38 is an official marine reserve, set aside to protect the endangered green and loggerhead turtles that come ashore on summer nights to hatch and bury their eggs.

Some 9km northeast of Pafos, the monastery of **Agios Neophytos** 39 (Áyios Neóphytos; stneophytos.org.cy; charge) dominates a wooded slope. Its church has fine sixteenth-century frescoes and icons, but the main focus is the twelfth-century **Enkleistra** (Hermitage), around which the monastery grew. The saintly historian and theologian Neophytos (1134–1219) supposedly hacked this cave-dwelling out of the rock with his own hands and then supervised the creation of the frescoes that decorate the chapel and cell. One shows Neophytos himself, being escorted into Paradise by two archangels.

On the north coast 35km from Pafos, the small town of **Polis** 40 stands where the ancient citykingdom of Marion once thrived from nearby gold and copper mines. Archaeological finds from the site are on display at the **Marion-Arsinoe Archaeological Museum** (26 322 955; charge). The old town centre has been restored and has a pleasant if touristy cluster of cafés and restaurants. Polis is a prelude to the fishing port and beach resort of **Latsii** (Latchí) ⓸⓵, where seafood tavernas cluster around the fishing port; to either side are decent sand-and-pebble beaches.

Romantics should head west to the end of the paved road, from where it's a brief stroll to the **Baths of Aphrodite** ⓸⓶, a small, shaded natural pool and springs set in a cool green glade, where the goddess was wont to bathe. Meatier hikes – either a coastal track giving swimming opportunities, or more challenging proper trails uphill – lead from here further into the **Akamas Peninsula**, one of the few unspoilt wildernesses left on the island and long a battleground between environmentalists and developers (see box below).

Northeast along the coast from Polis, a scenic route leads through relatively undeveloped seafront villages and past secluded beaches near **Pomos** and **Pachyammos** (Pahýammos). Beyond the latter, the road snakes through the steep hills of Tillyria to avoid the Turkish military enclave of Kokkina (Erenköy), before reaching the Cypriot-patronized resort of **Kato Pyrgos** ⓸⓷, no longer the end of the line since a crossing point to the North opened nearby.

Northern Cyprus

Highlights

- **The Mountain Castles**, see page 82
- **Keryneia (Girne)**, see page 84
- **West of Keryneia**, see page 85
- **Famagusta (Gazimağusa)**, see page 86
- **Salamis**, see page 87
- **The Karpasia Peninsula**, see page 37

The Turkish-occupied north, which comprises around 38 percent of the island, contains some of Cyprus' most beautiful landscapes, best beaches, most dramatic monuments and two of its most historic towns. Division and the subsequent political isolation long helped preserve the countryside from the ravages of mass tourism, but since 2000 development around Keryneia in particular has been every bit as intensive as anywhere in the South.

It is possible to whizz around Northern Cyprus in a day or two and cover – or at least glimpse – some of the main highlights, although unless you are short on time, this is not recommended. In three or four days you can see all the sights, including northern Nicosia (see page 46), at a more leisurely pace.

The castle ruins of Agios Ilarion

The Mountain Castles

North of Nicosia, the Mesaoria plain (Mesarya in Turkish) rises abruptly at the **Keryneia Hills**, which Lawrence Durrell, who lived in their shadow from 1953 to 1956, described as 'par excellence the Gothic range, for it is studded with crusader castles pitched on the dizzy spines of the mountains, commanding the roads which run over the saddles between'. The range's most striking peak is **Pentadaktylos** (Beşparmak, 'Five Fingers').

The three castles now lie in noble ruin, victims not of

VISITING THE NORTH

As of 2025, there are currently nine crossing-points along the buffer zone that separates North and South. There are two main pedestrian crossings in central Nicosia: Ledra/Lokmacı in the Old City and Ledra Palace nearby. Border crossings for vehicles are at Agios Dometios/Metehan in the western suburbs of Nicosia; at Pyla/Pergamos (Beyarmudu), handiest for Karpasia; direct to Famagusta (Gazimağusa); at Deryneia (Derynia), near Famagusta; at Astromeritis-Kato Zodeia (Boştancı), near Morfou (Güzelyurt); Kato Pyrgos (Günebakan) on the north coast and Lefka (Lefke) in the northwest.

The procedure for crossing is easy, though there can be long queues at weekends. Officially the border opens at 8am and closes for returning visitors at midnight, but the Nicosia crossings tend to be open almost around the clock. The Greek Cypriot police will view, but not stamp, your passport going in each direction; the Turkish Cypriot police will, upon request, give you a loose-leaf paper visa. They will stamp this paper visa, but make sure they do not stamp your passport, or you will be banned from re-entry to the South. There is no limit on the number of times you may cross. EU citizens have the right of unrestricted movement throughout Cyprus; there may be restrictions for non-EU citizens, especially coming from North to South.

Motorists going from South to North must buy supplemental insurance at the border, since no EU-contracted policies are valid in the Turkish Cypriot sector. The minimum term is three days, and the policies – with a low level of cover, and a record of not paying out compensation – are all but useless other than to wave at police. If you have an accident that immobilizes you in the North, get the car moving again without involving the car-hire company in the South – don't risk being stranded in the North.

enemy bombardment but of partial demolition by the Venetians. Most extensive is **Agios Ilarion** ㊹ (0533 161 276; charge), which climbs along knife-edge ridges in three tiers of battlements and towers, reaching an altitude of 670m under twin peaks, with steps leading up and down in all directions.

The castle was built in the tenth century around an earlier church and monastery honouring the hermit Hilarion, who fled here when the Arabs took Syria. The original Byzantine structure was fortified and extended by the Lusignans as a summer residence. The views down to Keryneia harbour are superb and, on a clear day, you can see the mountains of southern Turkey some 100km away.

Another dramatic, if small, ruinous castle is **Buffavento** 45 ('Buffeted by the Winds'; unrestricted access), just off the easterly major road over the Pentadaktylos. This is Cyprus' highest fortress, at 940m, with views over literally half the island, especially towards dusk when there's the spectacle of Nicosia turning on its lights.

Keryneia (Girne)

Offering the most beautiful sheltered harbour in Cyprus and a grand old castle, the charming town of **Keryneia** 46 – Girne in Turkish, still Kyrenia to most Greek Cypriots and expats – is the most strikingly situated on the island. The venerable buildings that line the port have almost all been converted into bars or restaurants of indifferent quality, but the setting is so irresistible that most every visitor patronizes them at least once.

Overlooking the harbour is massive **Keryneia Castle** (charge), whose fortifications date mostly from the Venetian era. Today, its walls enclose a Byzantine chapel, royal apartments and various historical displays, including the **Kyrenia ship**, the oldest wreck ever recovered from the seabed (and featured on three Cypriot euro coins). This Greek trading ship sank in 30m of water just offshore around 300 BC and was discovered in 1967 by a Greek-Cypriot diver. The surviving hull has been painstakingly preserved and remounted and is shown with part of its final cargo.

In the foothills behind Keryneia are the substantial ruins of the superbly sited Gothic abbey of **Bellapais** 47 (Beylerbeyi; 0392 815 75 40; charge). Facing the sea, the 'Abbaye de la Paix' (of which the current name is a corruption) stands on a 30m-high escarpment, its buildings enveloped in cypresses, palms and citrus trees. The abbey was built by Premonstratensian (Norbertine) brothers generously funded by Lusignan kings and took on its present form during the thirteenth and fourteenth centuries. The elegant cloister is adorned with finely carved figures, while the splendid, vaulted refectory has six bays and a fine rose window; underneath the refectory is a fine undercroft with 'palm' vaulting upholding the ceiling. The annual International North Cyprus Music Festival, see page 101, happens here in the autumn.

Bellapais Abbey

West of Keryneia

You can follow the line of the Pentadaktylos range west to their end and continue on through the main Maronite Catholic village of **Kormakitis** (Koruçam), enjoying something of a revival since 2003, with property being confidently renovated. The area is home to the Cyprus wild tulip; a protected flower that blossoms every spring. Southward around the curve of Morfou Bay is the old bishop's seat of **Morfou** 48 (Mórphou/Güzelyurt) and its venerable monastery of **Agios Mamas**), one of the few churches in the North still used (on feast days) for Orthodox worship, thanks to the efforts of the charismatic Bishop of Morfou, Neophytos.

On the narrow strip of Northern Cyprus squeezed between the buffer zone and the sea lie the remains of the sixth-century BC Graeco-Roman town of **Soloi** 49 (charge) and those of the Persian-era (fifth-century BC) palace at **Vouni** (Vuni; charge). Soloi is known for its fine mosaics, difficult to see except on bright days owing to a huge protective canopy.

Famagusta (Gazimağusa)

The east-coast port of **Famagusta** 50 (Ammochostos/Gazimağusa) was a mere village when Christian refugees arrived from Palestine in 1291. Soon it developed into a boomtown of extravagant merchants and notorious courtesans, becoming one of the wealthiest cities in the world. It all ended in late 1373 when the Genoese took the port as part of their general attacks across Cyprus. Worse was to come in 1571, with the Ottoman invasion and the most famous siege in the island's history.

Othello's Tower, Famagusta

Famagusta emerged during the twentieth century as the most important port in Cyprus and a major tourist centre. But once again, in 1974, a Turkish invasion was to leave the city a mere shadow of its former self. Since the departure of the Greek Cypriots, **Varosha** (Varosia/Varósha/Maraş), the pre-1974 beach resort area, is eerily deserted and decrepit. Its now-open neighbourhoods and Famagusta's Venetian fortifications and old town are still of great interest.

Beside the harbour stands the renovated **Othello's Tower** (charge), named after a sixteenth-century governor of Cyprus, Christoforo Moro, sometimes cited as the model for Shakespeare's tormented Moor. Most formidable of the fortifications is the **Martinengo Bastion** in the northwest corner of the old town. Its walls, 4–6m thick, provided stubborn resistance to the Ottomans during the siege of 1570–1.

The town's many churches were founded by the Lusignans. The finest was St Nicholas' Cathedral, where the Lusignan kings were crowned honorifically as kings of Jerusalem. It was converted into a mosque, the **Lala Mustafa Paşa Camii** (free), named after the commander of the Ottoman siege. The handsome structure was completed in 1326 with a majestic western facade modelled on Rheims cathedral. Although the Turks stripped the interior of any images of the human form, and there was damage from an earthquake in 1735, it still retains fine Gothic features.

Salamis

Overlooking the sea just 8km north of Famagusta, the ancient city of **Salamis** ➎➊ (00903788495; charge) rivals Kourion (see page 63) as the island's finest archaeological site. For almost 1,800 years, Salamis competed with Paphos as the leading city in Cyprus and was a haven for exiled Greek artists and intellectuals. Renamed Constantia, it became the capital of early-Christian Cyprus in about AD 350, subsequently suffering an earthquake and the silting up of its port; the city was abandoned after the Arab invasions.

The **Roman theatre** – tied for the largest in Cyprus, with the Nea Paphos theatre – seated 15,000. Also impressive is the spacious **gymnasium**. The graceful Corinthian columns of its **palaestra** were brought here from the theatre and re-erected by the

Sculpture in the ancient theatre at Salamis

Byzantines. In the adjoining **public baths**, you can distinguish the *frigidarium*, *tepidarium* and *caldarium* chambers. The water was channelled from Kythrea, 40km away, via a Roman aqueduct, parts of which are still standing. Check the ceiling vaults closely for superb mosaic fragments and frescoes, the latter clearly showing two figures reminiscent of Buddhist cave art.

Just west of Salamis is the monastery of **Apostolos Varnavas** 52 (charge). He accompanied Paul on his mission to Cyprus in AD 45 and was martyred in Salamis at the hands of Jews he was trying to convert. The saint's rock-cut subterranean burial chamber (free entry) is now empty, but its discovery in AD 478 helped the Church of Cyprus achieve autonomy within the Orthodox faith and led to the building of the monastery nearby. The present drum-domed church was built in 1756 with elements from an earlier fifteenth-century church and columns and capitals from Salamis. It is now a museum of mediocre post-Byzantine icons; more worthwhile is an extensive archaeological gallery, the North's largest, in the building just behind.

The Karpasia Peninsula

By overnighting in the North, you'll be able to make a long, exhilarating drive into the 'panhandle' of the Karpasia (Karpaz) Peninsula.

Don't try this on a day-trip – the distances are enormous and, despite improvements, the road network still too challenging.

The peninsula can be said to start at the castle of **Kantara** ❺❸, the easternmost and most intact of the Byzantine-Lusignan castles of the Pentadaktylos range (charge). Even at its base, Karpasia is so narrow that the citadel was able to simultaneously survey both its north and south coasts. Tradition places the surrender of Isaac Komnenos to Richard the Lionheart here in 1191.

The main peninsular trunk road reaches the north coast just past Aigialousa (Yenierenköy); immediately after, in the village of **Agias Trias** ❺❹ (Sipahi), is a fifth-century **Christian basilica** containing some of the finest floor mosaics on Cyprus, probably executed by the same craftsmen responsible for those at Kourion and Nea Paphos. They are mostly geometric, except for a peculiar motif of paired sandals – possibly symbolic of the journey through this world to the next.

Continue east to **Dipkarpaz (Rizokarpaso)** ❺❺, Karpasia's largest village and a curiosity in that about 230 Greek Orthodox continue to live here; bypassed by the invasion, they were never forcibly expelled but did endure extremely hard times until 2003. There's food and lodging along the road between here and **Agios Filon (Ayfilon)**, the site of ancient Karpasia, of which only a large, half-intact basilica, romantically flanked by palm trees, remains. A little west extends an excellent beach, known as **Dipkarpaz Halk Plajı**. Some 18km beyond is another stunning beach, Cyprus' best: **Nangomi** ('Golden Beach') ❺❻, where rustic dune-top bungalows inland constitute the only real backpacker 'resort' on the island. You've probably seen 5,000m-long 'Golden Beach' already, as it figures in almost every northern Cypriot tourism promotional poster.

Last stop, near Karpasia's stormy tip, is the much-venerated monastery of **Apostolos Andreas** ❺❼. The extensive restoration works have been completed and so the site is now open to visitors and worshippers.

Diving at the Zenobia shipwreck

Things to do

Cyprus offers plenty to do beyond sightseeing. Sporting activities benefit from a great climate and clear coastal waters, while entertainment ranges from loud music festivals to more sedate dance presentations or concerts in an ancient open-air amphitheatre or vaulted medieval building.

Outdoor activities

Most of Cyprus' beaches, with crystal clear waters, offer a unique setting for watersports that both families and adventure junkies can enjoy. Further inland, hikers can find solitude and marvellous scenery in the unspoilt Troödos and Pentadaktylos mountains, or on the rugged Akamas Peninsula. Golf courses exist around the island, whilst in the winter months, the slopes of Troödos even offer skiing.

Watersports

Scuba divers and **snorkellers** are major beneficiaries of Cyprus' limpid seas. Submerged cliffs, valleys and caves are easy to explore offering close-up views of sea anemones, sponges and crustaceans (although colourful fish are not abundant in the nutrient-poor eastern Mediterranean). In Protaras, try Green Bay Watersports (www.greenbaywake.com).

You can also dive over several wrecks, best of all the 1980 ferry *Zenobia*, or at Ayia Napa's MUSAN Museum of Underwater Sculpture. You will find certified diving centres with equipment for hire and instruction at Pafos, Coral Bay, Latsi, Larnaka, Limassol, Agia Napa and Protaras in the South, and at Keryneia (Girne) in the North. One particularly good outfitter for the *Zenobia* wreck is Larnaka- and Limassol-based Dive-In (www.dive-in.com.cy).

Windsurfing is widely practiced, though conditions are best around Pervolia, and Episkopi Bay; equipment can be hired at public and hotel beaches. Head to Kahuna Surfhouse in Kiti for chill vibes, classes, competitions and social activities (www.kahuna surfhouse.eu) **Jet-skiing** and **parasailing** are available at the main resorts. Those serious about **sailing** can hire craft from the harbours at Agia Napa, Pafos, Ltsi, Larnaka, Limassol and Keryneia.

Golf

Golf is not a game much associated with Cyprus, but five excellent courses in the South are worth seeking out: **Secret Valley**, tucked away not far from Petra tou Romiou; **Aphrodite Hills** close by; **Minthis**, in Tsada; and **Vikla** and **Elias** near Limassol. There is also the new Limassol Greens Golf. The North has courses at Pentageia (Yeşilyurt) and Agios Amvrosios (Esentepe).

Walking and hiking

The Troödos Mountains and Akamas Peninsula are ideal for hiking, though for most people it will be too uncomfortable in summer. The tourism organisation, Visit Cyprus, has maps and information on local itineraries (see page 140). Visit the Pafos or Polis offices for the Akamas Peninsula, and the Pano Platres office for the Troödos Mountains. Ask at any tourist office for the excellent *Nature Trails* brochure, which maps out around twenty walks all over the south of the island.

Adjacent to the Baths of Aphrodite car park, there's a tourism board placard that has details of walking trails; from here paths lead off into the Akamas – with the exception of the unmissable traverse of the Avakas Gorge, reached from the peninsula's southwest shore.

NOTES

In winter, three drag-lifts and a chair-lift provide access to eight ski runs on Mt Olympos' northeast slopes. Depending on snow conditions, the ski season lasts from January to late March. Check current conditions on www.cyprus ski.com.

Hiking in the Troödos mountains

In the North, the Pentadaktylos Mountains look tempting, but few proper trails exist – only 4x4 tracks.

The most popular nature trails in the Troödos are the Atalante and Artemis ones around Mt Olympos, and the shorter hikes up to Kaledonia Falls or out to Makrya Kontarka along the 6.5km-long Persephone trail, but better and more unspoilt is the loop route around Madari (Madhári) ridge, with the most accessible trailhead (and best parking) near Kyperounta (Kyperoúnda).

Horseriding

There are a dozen reputable stables or riding clubs in the South, mostly around Limassol, Pafos and the outskirts of Nicosia, as horseriding (during the cooler months) has grown in popularity. The Travellers Handbook lists them all; one to single out for rural

Skiing is popular in the Troödos mountains

landscapes and group activities is Lythrodontas Riding Club (www. lythrodontasridingclub.com)

Extreme sports

Cliff jumping is popular along the coast of Agia Napa, though it should be done with caution. Alternatively, Agia Napa's **Slingshot**, claims to be the highest and fastest ride in the world. Riders are propelled to a height of 100m in a breathtaking 1.3 seconds. **Tandem paragliding** is a spectacular option from the coast of Protaras and the palisades of the hills above Keryneia (Girne).

If you fancy a spot of mountain biking, there's plenty of testing dirt tracks in the Troödos and Pentadaktylos mountains, on the Akamas Peninsula, around Cape Gkreko and in the wilds of Tillyria, Pitsilia and Karpasia. Take plenty of water and don't overdo it in summer.

Shopping

The quality of many tourist shops in Cyprus is low, tending towards cheap, imported wares. Head instead for the nearest **Cyprus Handicraft Service** (CHS) shop, (a renovated one opened at the Nicosia headquarters in September 2025) showcasing the best of the island's artisans in an attempt to revive traditional folk art. Goods here are comparatively expensive, but they are handmade and have the CHS label to guarantee it. You will find CHS shops at **Limassol**: Themidos 25 and **South Nicosia**: CHS workshop, Leoforos Athalassis 186 (www.cyprushandicraft.gov.cy).

You can also find the works of talented craftspeople in various fields in their own shops, in Nicosia explore the art studios on Ermou street and in Limassol's old town browse the local artist shops near Ankara street

The gift shops of many of the South's museums – in particular the Cyprus Museum in Nicosia, and the Pierides in Larnaka have remarkable, if pricier, objects. For franchises, head to the American-style malls. Nicosia has three, Paphos two and Limassol and Larnaca each have one.

Best buys

Handmade crafts. Cypriot artists make excellent basketry items - from small baskets or trays, *tsésti*, in decorative shapes and colours to large articles in rush or cane. Red clay is popular in local ceramics and a boom in the industry means that you'll easily find stunning pieces with traditional designs. If in Lekfara, pick up the hand stitched and renowned lefkaritiko embroidery. Choose from linen tablecloths, doilies, runners, umbrellas, hand fans and handkerchiefs. Iconography is also big on the island and you'll find plenty of pieces by highly skilled monastic artists.

Copperware. After three millennia, the copper industry remains a source of Cypriot pride. There is all manner of hand-crafted wares, including pots, saucepans and bowls.

A basket weaver at work

Food and wine. Top of the list is of course halloumi, then a sweet, jelly-like confection, *loukoúmi*, or 'Cyprus Delight', which is a speciality of Geroskipou. The Turkish version, *lokum*, or 'Turkish Delight', is sold in the North. Well-sealed packets of *loúntza* (cured pork loin) travel well, as do carefully wrapped bottles of *teratzómelo* (carob syrup). Of the many wines and liqueurs produced in Cyprus, the most popular gift is the fortified, amber-coloured sweet dessert wine Commandaria. For last-minute buys, Larnaka airport's Cyprus section sells these.

Jewellery. If lucky, you'll stumble upon a local jewellery designer on a walk. Otherwise, many of the excellent designers are now featured in hotel shops presenting pieces inspired by Cyprus. Do check if sterling silver carries the 925 hallmark.

Leather goods. Manufactured locally, shoes and sandals are reasonably priced in Cyprus.

Culture

Cyprus is becoming a year-round destination with off-season festivals, growing university life for locals and internationals, picturesque Christmas stays, performances from acclaimed global art companies and a rising music production industry. All this, alongside the country's traditional festivities.

Art

Art exhibitions run year-round, the majority of them in Limassol and Nicosia. Larnaca, a previously quiet town, has re-entered the art scene largely thanks to the establishment of Larnaca Biennale (biennalelarnaca.com) – a bi-annual event happening in the fall of 2025 and 2027 and so on, hosting local and global artists. Post-covid, the arts were shown greater importance with more state-sponsored funds and artists opening studios offering workshops – particularly ceramic.

Comedy

This may be surprising to many but Cyprus has a growing stand-up scene (www.motioncomedy.com) and even has a Cyprus Comedy Festival and a Laughter Festival. Local comedians now have TV shows, organise open mic nights and the scene has even welcomed internationally-acclaimed comedians such as Jimmy Carr, Russell Peters and Bill Bailey performing live in English. Greece's top comedians also frequently tour southern Cyprus.

Music

The local live scene is buzzing, particularly with jazz and rock bands, and of course Greek folk singers who perform every weekend. Nicosia has a dedicated jazz venue, Sarah's Jazz Club, (Xanthis Xenierou, 35; www.sarahsjazzclub.com) whilst Paphos' Technopolis 20 (Nikolaou I. Nikolaidi Avenue 18, www.technopolis20.com) is an excellent cultural venue for recitals, exhibitions and markets. Larnaka's The Tudor Inn Bar & Restaurant (Lala Moustafa Pashia, 6026) often hosts live music nights on the weekends. The Limassol Music Hall, (Georgiou A' Ave 89, Yermasoyia) along with Rialto Theatre (Andrea Drousioti 19), host weekly shows as well. For a taste of something different, Batukinio Percussion Band is a street drumming group that plays Afro-Brazilian music particularly during the Limassol carnival.

NIGHTLIFE

Cyprus' nightlife scene has drastically upgraded from the rather-sketchy clubs of Ayia Napa. Though these are still popular with the youth (Castle Club and Black N White in particular), stylish beach bars bring a different kind of fun. Guaba (7 Amathuntos; guababeachbar.com) in Limassol is popular amongst the locals, as is Serena Bay (115 Vrysoudion; www.serena.com.cy) and Riva (52 Ayias Theklas; www.rivabeachouse.com) in Paralimni and Ayia Napa respectively which offer more dressed-up seaside parties. There are also award-winning restaurants and cocktail bars to discover. Nicosia was awarded the Best Beverage Experience for Culinary Travellers and a Culinary Capital in 2024 and its Lost + Found Drinkery (38 Lord Byron Street) is in the world's top 50 bars. For lovers of electronic music, BEONIX Festival in Limassol (Sept; www.beonix.art) and Music Element (www.musicelement.com) in Paralimni are the biggest techno events on the island.

Several bars in northern Nicosia's old town host live music nights as well and the coastal cities with summer music festivals.

Theatre, dance and film

There's a diverse performance art scene on the island. From folklore shows and festivals in villages and the seaside (check the Mediterranean Folklore Festival in Larnaka every September) to the Dervish and belly dancing in norther Cyprus. The Cyprus Theatre Organisation (www.thoc.org.cy) hosts monthly productions in Greek, whilst the Anglo-Cypriot Theatre does plays in English and smaller groups present plays in Russian. The Nicosia International Festival stages impressive cultural productions whilst Limassol's Rialto Theatre hosts some of the biggest festivals such as the Cyprus Choreography Platform (Nov; www.cyprus choreographyplatform.com).

Of the most impressive venues to catch a performance is the Ancient Kourion Theatre, the Ancient Pafos Odeion, (where the

International Festival of Ancient Greek Drama is hosted in the summer), the Olive Grove in Delikipos and Bellapais Abbey.

Cyprus for children

With clean beaches and endless sunshine, Cyprus is great for children (but be sure to protect them from the fierce Mediterranean sun). Cypriots, like most southern Europeans, love children and there are few, if any, restrictions on where they can go.

If the kids are bored with the beach, but not with the water, there are four water parks to experience. **WaterWorld** (www.waterworldwaterpark.com), just west of Agia Napa at Agia Thekla, claims to be the biggest themed park in Europe, with over twenty

Making a splash from the sea slides

Greek-mythology-themed rides, ranging from high-speed thrill chutes to the Lazy River. There are two other water parks in the South: **Watermania** (www.fasouri-watermania.com) in Limassol. The **Paphos Aphrodite Waterpark** (www.aphroditewaterpark.com) between Pafos and Geroskipou also has its superlatives, including a long rafting ride.

The biggest and best amusement park is **Paliatso Fun Fair Luna Park** (www.parkopaliatsocy.com) in Agia Napa. Fun fairs are also mounted every Christmas in downtown Nicosia and Larnaca (23 724744).

Calendar of events

6 January *Ta Fota*. On Epiphany Day, bishops bless the waters in seaside towns, throwing a crucifix into the sea to be recovered by divers.

February/March *Carnival*. Limassol's 10-day long celebration features fancy-dress balls and a final-Saturday parade. It's not Rio, but it is fun.

April/May *Easter*. Good Friday eve sees solemn liturgies everywhere, following by the parading of the *Epitafios* (Christ's Bier). The Saturday midnight *Anastasi* (Resurrection) service has the congregation lighting their candles from the priest's, followed by a bonfire *Cyprus Film Days* (www.cyprusfilmdays.com). Nine-day festival of the best new global cinema, mostly at Limassol's Rialto Theatre and Nicosia's Zena Palace Cinema.

May/June *Pharos International Chamber Music Festival*. A week of top-drawer concerts at breath-taking locations. (www.pharosartsfoundation.org). *Kataklysmos*. The Festival of the Flood is an important public holiday with folklore performances, water games and music concerts.

July Windcraft Music Fest. Live music performances and art workshops at Katydata village (www.windcraftmusicfest.com).

August *Paradise Jazz Festival*. A weekend of jazz at Paradise Place in Pomos (www.paradisejazzfestival.com).

Carnival time in Limassol

15 August *Dormition of the Virgin*. The faithful gather in massive crowds at the leading monasteries and churches.
September *Limassol Wine Festival*. Twelve days of wine tastings, dancing and folklore shows. Mediterranean Folklore Festival. Choirs, folklore dance ensembles from Cyprus and the region perform at Finikoudes seafront.
September/October *International North Cyprus Music Festival*. (www.facebook.com/InternationalNorthCyprusMusicFestival) A festival of chamber and choral music and dance in Bellapais Abbey, one of north Cyprus's most beautiful settings.
October *Ayia Napa Medieval Festival*. Marching bands, folklore performances and flag-bearers perform live. Nicosia Book Fest. Annual literature festival with activities for all ages (www.nicosiabookfest.com).

Food and drink

For Cypriots, enjoying and making good food comes naturally. Cyprus is a foodies' paradise and the local food scene has seen a change since Covid times. Long gone are the clutter of touristy seafront restaurants serving frozen food (though some still linger – you've been warned). Now, local chefs make Cypriot produce and wild-grown ingredients (like *kolokasi*; taro root or carob) the stars of the show in an attempt to highlight cuisine that is inspired by the island and its people.

Many flavours are still greatly influenced by Greece, Turkey and the Middle East, whilst there has also been a growth of excellent international restaurants in the south, and not the world buffet kind. Stylish eateries serving Thai, *Nikkei* cuisine, gourmet Mediterranean, smash burgers and Neapolitan doughy pizza have popped up – some are even award-winning.

For a truly delectable meal, you might break the bank – food & drink costs have increased – yet a few humble taverns, spotted by their traditional domed oven and *bougainvillea* trees, have remained that will serve you hearty food without leaving you penniless. It's easy to eat well in Cyprus; after all it is one of the locals' favourite past-times.

Where to eat

Cyprus has a varied culinary scene with eateries of all types, for all tastes and hours of the day. Tavernas are typically informal, even rustic, and are traditional eating and drinking establishments. The maeirkó, or casserole-food kitchen, cheaply dishing out full, home-style meals, are popular local joints, open typically for lunch. Another type of eatery is the mezé house, similar to a taverna, known as a meyhane in the north. They serve a set menu of what seems like never-ending food. Always order for one person less than the number of diners.

A modern eatery in Limassol

Souvlatzidika are humble grill houses that have mastered the art of souvlaki and sheftelia or other charcoal-grilled meats. These don't normally serve the Greek gyros served in warm pitta, you'll have to go to a gyradiko for that which won't be hard to find as locals love them.

Apart from the fast-food chains, bakeries are a hotspot in Cyprus, often serving as places to bump into acquaintances and have a good catch-up. They are literally pastry heaven and most of the bigger ones also serve good, fresh coffee. The 24-hour ones double up as after-hours joints for revellers returning from a night out on the town.

In some towns, you'll find food trucks serving falafel wraps, fried chicken or grilled sandwiches. Stylish brunch spots are also on the rise – either dishing out a Cypriot breakfast of village bread, halloumi, sausages, olives and tomatoes or American-style eggs and pancakes. Meanwhile, the place to meet locals is at café-bars and wine bars, where they enjoy sitting for hours chatting over coffee, beer or bubbly.

Top 10 things to try

1. Halloumi/hellim

Look out for halloumi, goat- or ewe's-milk cheese soaked in brine. Rubbery when raw, and even lovelier when fried or grilled.

2. Tahini & taramosaláta dips

More popular in Cyprus than tzatziki is tahini, a sesame seeds dip mixed with lemon juice, olive oil and garlic. *Taramosaláta* is a light pink fish-roe paste made with olive oil and lemon juice, thickened with mashed potato or breadcrumbs. A good one will be more white and creamy rather than bright pink, which indicates it is loaded with processed ingredients.

3. Koúpes

A snack shared with neighbouring countries, Cypriots love this torpedo-shaped fried bite. The outer layer is deep fried bulgur wheat stuffed with onions and mincemeat or mushrooms for vegetarians.

4. Village salad

An adaptation of the Greek salad, this includes lettuce or cabbage, cucumber, tomatoes, olives, and always a thick slice or two of feta cheese. It is considered a must-eat, waiters might not even ask if you want one and it'll simply arrive on the table.

5. Mixed grill

A souvlakia and sheftalia combo (charcoal-grilled kebab and mince-meat sausage) typically served in pitta bread with tomatoes, cucumbers and onions with some sauces. To order it, just ask for 'mia pitta mix'.

6. Stifado

This is one of the most famous meat stews in Cyprus. It was traditionally made with very tender rabbit meat, but nowadays more often features beef. It is made with red wine onions and peppercorns and is served with rice.

7. Koupépia/yaprak dolması and gemista

Vine leaves stuffed with rice and lamb, flavoured with mint, different from the Greek equivalent dolmades that are vegetarian. *Gemista* are stuffed vegetables.

Traditional souvlaki

8. Afélia

A tender pork stew made with red wine, cumin and coriander seeds. It is typically served with oven potatoes or a tomato-based bulgur wheat and pairs well with a dollop of yoghurt; most commonly eaten at night.

9. Kleftiko

Although it is a heavy meat dish, the summer months is when this slow-oven-baked dish is served. The tender lamb meat is cooked for at least six to eight hours.

10. Makaronia tou fournou

Literally translating as 'pasta baked in the oven', this dish layers thick pasta tubes with minced meat, béchamel sauce and cheese. The

Cypriot version differs from the Greek *pastitsio* in that it uses dried mint and cinnamon.

Cypriot specialities

What is considered authentic local cuisine, beyond the hearty meat dishes, is typically simple, everyday food Cypriots eat at home that you'll find in traditional tavernas or *maeirka*. *Kolokási/bules*, is one of them; taro root, diced and cooked in a tomato-based stew with meat or chicken. *Louviá/Bürülce* (black-eyed peas) are best enjoyed with hefty drizzles of olive oil and lemon and are commonly eaten during lunchtime with a slice of bread and tinned tuna or sardines. A big part of everyday Cypriot cuisine is

Grilled octopus

also fresh *goutsiá/bakla* (broad beans) and *bámies/bamya* (okra, lady fingers).

Cypriot ravioli (*Kypriakes ravioles/pirohu*) are warm, soft and stuffed with halloumi and mint, and enjoyed with grated anari cheese. In Lefkara village, you will find the most renowned version of the *ttavás/dava* dish – a sweetish, onion-laden, clay-pot stew, usually of lamb with cubed potatoes, cumin-flavoured rice and vegetables. Look out for *shiromeri* (cured pork), *ortíchia/bıldırcın* (roast quail) or *karaolous* (casserole snails) in a tomato sauce.

Vegetarian dishes

Traditional Cypriot cuisine is not particularly vegetarian-friendly. At best, you'll be served a plate of grilled vegetables, halloumi, dips and salad. A taverna might also have zesty *kolokithokeftedes* (courgette fritters) or *kolokouthkia me ta afk*a (courgette with eggs).

In spring and summer; two tasty local dishes that also happen to be vegetarian are *anthoi gemistoi* – stuffed courgette flowers with a rice-tomato-garlic mix, and *poulles*, a taro root-like vegetable that tastes similar to a potato; they come fried, and sprinkled with salt and oregano.

More contemporary local dining establishments will have vegetarian meals, though, as eateries try to cater for all diets. The international cuisine that now exists on the island serves meat, vegetarian and vegan meals. In the main towns, particularly in Nicosia, Larnaka and Pafos, there are exclusive vegetarian café-restaurants that make fresh, colourful dishes daily.

Fish and shellfish

The fishing village of Zygi has plenty of fish tavernas, continued along the Paralimni-Protaras coast and the northern Karpasia Peninsula. Several big fish houses are spread around the island, yet not all serve fresh fish – look out for an asterix that signals a frozen food menu. it's best to ask what the fresh fish of the day is.

A perfect Greek salad

Octopus *(khtapódi/ahtapod)* is served in a red wine sauce, or grilled. Prawns *(karídes/karides)* or battered squid *(kalamarákia/kalamar)* are other common menu items. Prawns saganaki is a hot tomato sauce dish with melted feta cheese on top.

For fried fish, try red mullet (*parpoúni/tekir*), whitebait (*marídes/smirida*) or atherina. Large fish like sea bass and sea bream are typically fresh. In Kakopetria, do try the farmed trout (*pestrofa*), fried or grilled.

Desserts and sweets

Dessert is taken as seriously as main meals in Cyprus and most sweets are drizzled in some sort of natural syrup. *Daktyla*, or Ladies' fingers, is a crispy almond fried pastry with cinnamon, sugar and orange blossom water syrup. *Lokoumades*, fried pastry balls dough in syrup are made on the spot and are best enjoyed hot after lunch or as an afternoon snack. You'll rarely find them in the evening unless at a village fair in the summer.

Spoon sweets (*glyká tou koutaliou/macun*) are preserved candied fruits or even vegetables – which can mean oranges, green walnuts, cherries, watermelons or grapes. Enjoy them with a traditional coffee in the afternoon. *Soutzoukos/Sujuk* is one of the most popular desserts in Cyprus, made of grapes and usually served with coffee and tea.

Honey and nuts are used in both *baklavás*/baklava, layered filo pastry, and *kataïfi/kadayıf*, filaments resembling shredded wheat. Less cloyingly sweet and more genuinely Cypriot are *palouzé* (grape juice pudding) and *mahallebí/muhallebi* (cherry-pit flour and rosewater pudding). For a lighter note, indulge in the island's seasonal fruit – loquats, strawberries, guavas, citrus, grapes, figs, watermelon, Persian melons, plums and cherries.

Coffee

The traditional local coffee is generic oriental style, served sweet *(glykó/şekerli)*, medium-sweet *(métrio/orta)*, or without sugar *(skéto/sade)*, accompanied by a glass of cool water. Do not disturb or drink the thick sediment at the bottom of the cup. Iced coffee is also popular in Cyprus and has moved away from the frappé (whipped cold instant coffee) and adopted Greece's freddo espresso culture – espresso shots whisked with ice.

MEALTIMES AND ETIQUETTE

Meals tend to last several hours in Cyprus, used as a time to catch up. Breakfast, depending on the establishment type, can be served from 7am to 12pm. Lunch usually begins at 1pm, though you'll rarely find Cypriots tucking in before 1.30–2pm. To cater to travellers, most kitchens open at 12pm and serve almost throughout the day, with the exception perhaps of a few hours in the afternoon.

You can have dinner from around 7pm onwards and be served until 10pm or 11pm at night. Most locals make their reservations around 8.30–9.30pm though, especially in the summer to avoid the heat. It is best to call and book a table if staying in a crowded area and restaurants tend to fill up quickly, all-year-round.

When it comes to tipping, it is expected – usually about 10 percent of the total food bill. If having only drinks, a couple of euros is generally satisfactory.

Bitter orange spoon sweets

Alcohol

Cyprus' amber-coloured sweet dessert wine Commandaria is considered to be the oldest in the world, originally produced for the Knights of St John at Kolossi. Lovers of sweet and sherry-type wines will have plenty of local flavours to taste on the island. Dotted in the villages are picturesque wineries that provide for the country like Vlassides Winery in Limassol, Tsiakkas in Pelendri, and Vouni in Panagia. Linos in Omodos remarkably created Cyprus' first blue natural wine – it's impressive, yet not the tastiest. In the North, most wine is imported from Turkey, with the exception of bottles from a single microwinery, Château St-Hilarion.

As an after-dinner drink, you may be offered a *zivanía,* the local fire water, distilled from grape-pressing residue. The beer industry has grown beyond the national KEO, Leon or Turkish Efes in the north. Sandy and Humour beers are locally produced while Pivo Microbrwery on the outskirts of Nicosia is a popular and well respected craft beer brand.

In the summer, Cyprus' signature cocktail – Brandy Sour – is popular. It's a refreshing brandy-based drink with angostura bitters, lemonade and soda. There's a debate going on whether mint should be included or not. It's cooling and cheaper than the cosmopolitan cocktails.

To help you order...

Could we have a table? **Boroúme na éhoume éna trapézi?**
I'd like a/an/some… **Tha íthela…**
I'm a vegetarian **Íme hortofágos**
The bill, please **To logariazmó, parakaló**
plate **piáto**
cutlery **maheropírouna**
glass **potíri**
bread **psomí**
butter **voútyro**
salt **aláti**
black pepper **mávro pipéri**
Cheers! **Giámas!**
Bon appétit! **Kalí órexi**!
Good continuation! (to the next course) **Kalí synéhia!**

Menu reader

fried **tiganitó**
roasted **psitó**
fish **psári**
meat **kréas**
beef **vodinó**
goat **katsíki**
chicken **kotópoulo**
lamb **arní**
salad **saláta**
aubergine/eggplant **melitzána**
potatoes **patátes**
rice **rýzi, piláfi**
A litre/half litre **Éna litro/misó litro**
wine **krasí**
beer **býra**
mineral water **metallikó neró**
coffee **kafés**
tea **tsái**
milk **gala**
sugar **záhari**
dessert **glykó, epidórpio**
fruit **froúta**
ice cream **pagotó**

Places to eat

We have used the following symbols to give an idea of the per-person price for a three-course meal (or a mezé), excluding drinks:
€ = under 20 euros
€€ = 20-30 euros
€€€ = 30-50 euros
€€€€ = over 50 euros

Southern Cyprus

Nicosia

Evroulla Stoa Klokkari, old town; 22 665346. Sandwiched between Ledras and Onasagorou Streets is *Evroulla*, which has been serving traditional Cypriot cuisine since 1988. There is a different menu every day of dishes cooked to order and despite being in the busy, historical centre, it has not lost its quality – the hand-cut fries are proof. **€€**

Kathodon Lidras 62D; 22 661656. Just 100m from the checkpoint, this place is enduringly popular with trendy Cypriots and discerning foreigners. The menu is Cypriot and mainland Greek fusion, either *mezé* format or à la carte, though wine choice is limited. Seating is on the ground floor, on a small loft or outside; satirical maxims and photos of film/music stars line the walls. There's quality acoustic Greek music most nights; come for the buzz as much as for the grub. Bookings essential at weekends. **€€**

Pantopoleio Metochiou; 38, www.pantopoleiocy.com. Since 2010, this taverna has gained a loyal following for fare straddling metropolitan Greek and Cypriot in the best possible way. Heaping salads or starters like sausages with leeks, *pink grapefruit* salad or deep fried halloumi precede mains such as pork chops garnished with tzatziki tip. Save room for decadent desserts like mousse with orange zest, or *ekmek kantaifi*. Pavement tables are always packed during warm weather; the 1920s interior, recalling its past as a grocery *(pandopolío)*, can get noisy. **€€€**

Sawa Klimentos 31, Agios Antonios district, new town; sawasyrianrestaurant.com. One of two excellent Syrian restaurants in the capital, Sawa is popular with families who know good value when they see it. If the kitsch interior is too much, dine out in the garden (where a heated tent is erected in winter). It would be masochistic to have mains, when the *mezé*/salad platters are so rich – loaded with *nakanek* (sausage), *fattoush* (salad made with fried pita), tabbouli and *sodat dajaj* (chicken livers), among others. For dessert, try *mahallebí* or *baklavás*, neither overly sweet nor gooey. For a tipple, there's *arak* or *ouzo* to any measure, cheaper than the still-competitive wine list. Private parking is a plus in this congested area. **€€**

Tocayo Prevezis 10, new town; www.cesorogroup.com. Continuing the island's passion with sharing plates on the table is this stylish restaurant that pioneers Nikkei cuisine; a blend of Latin American and Peruvian flavours. Its prawn risotto and crispy nori salmon are must-tries, as well as the signature cocktails. **€€€**

Zanettos Trikoúpi 65, old town; 22 765501. A modest entrance leads to this arcaded warren, going strong since 1938, with wall photos of past illustrious patrons staring down at you (except in the indoor summer patio). Despite its fame among foreigners, quality has been maintained, with a loyal local following. Tuck into the monstrously large set-price *mezé*, which might include snails, wine-marinated spare ribs, sliced liver, bean dishes, or *pourgoúri* (bulgur wheat) with noodles. Dessert (if you've got room) comprises of *mahallebí*, fruit and *halvás*. The Pafos bulk wine is decent. **€€**

Larnaka

Art Café 1900 Stasinou 6; 24 653027. This charming bar-restaurant occupies a lovely early-twentieth-century townhouse near the Pierides

Museum. Downstairs, among film posters on the walls, it serves a large selection of beers (especially Belgian) and whiskies, plus expertly segued classic rock. Upstairs, there's a Mediterranean-fusion restaurant, with dishes like chicken with orange, thyme and garlic; duck on special occasions and vegetarian options. Wall decor consists of original canvases (by several artists)while there may be apple crumble for dessert. **€€**

Glykolemono Zinonos Kitieos 105; 24 623010. Larnaka's favourite, and classiest, café, with Belle Epoque floor tiles but otherwise contemporary decor. Besides expertly brewed coffees, the stock in trade is specialty pastries like *peïnirlí* and sweet or savoury *bougátsa* (custard pie), a great breakfast, big salads and fairly good pizzas. **€€**

Militzis 42 Piyale Pasa; www.militzis.com A hugely popular (with Cypriots as well as visitors) traditional Greek-Cypriot restaurant just beyond the fort on busy sea-lapped Piyale Pasa, *Militzis* is hard to miss – there's a big wind-pump wreathed in climbing plants at the front, and an industrial-scale clay oven at the back. The roasted and grilled meats are out of this world, the service is excellent, and the prices are very reasonable. Book early if you want to sit out on the terrace. **€€**

Psarolimano Piale Paşa 118; www.psarolimano.com. Set on Larnaka's fishing harbour with fine views of the sea, this popular restaurant has been operating in the same place since 1975. The menu leans towards fish and seafood – always fresh, caught locally – and fish *mezé*. Excellent food, excellent value. **€€€**

To Patriko Archiepiskopou Makariou; 99 870998. In the Larnaca district in Tersefanou village is the award-winning To Patriko, one of the only restaurants to serve Cypriot fine dining. They specialise in using raw, wild, local ingredients to re-introduce traditional dishes with a contemporary twist. There's a set menu with a description explaining the thought behind each dish and an extra nice touch, all plates are served by one of the two siblings that own it (the third is the chef). Look out for the Cyprus-shaped dessert. An expensive but unique dining experience. **€€€€**

Zephyros Piale Paşa 37; 24 657198. The most reliably performing of several fish tavernas along here, with a tellingly high level of local patronage. Scaly fish or cephalopods come with the traditional *tsayíri* garnish rather than a formal salad: in springtime, likely to be celery, *kouloúmbra*, raw artichokes, lettuce, parsley and rocket. An army of black-and-white-liveried waiters provide an efficient service. **€€-€€€**

Agia Napa and around

Demetrion Limanaki, Potamos Liopetriou; 99 323403. The more seaward of the two tavernas here, the smell of fresh fish and hand-cut chips frying in fresh oil tells you you've come to the right place. Avoid the cheaper seafood 'portions', which tend to be farmed species; go for by-weight offerings, which are likely to be landed at the adjacent anchorage. Seating inside or out on the terrace, it's a pleasantly breezy spot when the rest of the island is baking. Service is fairly efficient, despite habitual Cypriot crowds. **€€-€€€**

Ploumin 28 Oktovriou 3, Sotira; 99 658333. Well-signed in the village centre, this listed building from 1938 features a double-arched interior with lithographs, old film stills, posters and pottery as decor, while old tools adorn the summer patio. The *mezé* changes seasonally – interesting dishes like *kolokássia* (taro root) with lamb or fennel mushrooms may be 'off' – but rabbit is usually available. Bulk wine is from Statós village, or there's a well-stocked cellar. Live music two nights weekly. **€€**

Stamna Dimokratias, Apia Napa; www.stamnatavern.com. This little taverna is set in a stone house dating from the 1900s – Agia Napa's oldest house according to the owners. And with its gloriously crumbling stone and sun-faded shutters, it certainly has a lived-in charm. Expect good-value traditional Cypriot fare, and its *taramosaláta* and *mezé* deserves a special mention. The dishes are delicious, the service warm and welcoming. **€€**

Taverna Kamasias Daidalou 23, Paralimnitel; 23 825144. This minimally signposted taverna is best in winter or spring, when seasonal delicacies like *agrélia* (asparagus) with eggs, wild mushrooms, fresh fish and game platters join usual offerings like lamb liver, mussel risotto and heaping salads. Both à la carte and *mezé* options are available, and there's a well-stocked cellar of Greek and Cypriot micro-winery labels. The light stone-clad interior is more inspiring than the narrow terrace outside – another good reason to come off-season. **€€€**

Limassol (Lemesos) and around

Artima Bistro Carob Mill Complex Queen Berengaria Street; www.carobmill-restaurants.com. One of the cluster of restaurants and bars in the atmospheric Carob Mill Complex behind the castle. Stylish Italian/Mediterranean and award-winning food in spacious bistro surroundings, with additional tables outside and on an internal balcony. Try the rack of lamb or the lobster ravioli. **€€€€**

Hill View Restaurant and Apartments Stadiou 60, Pissouri; www.hillview.com.cy. A family-run restaurant with a chic interior, breathtaking views and a lovely terrace. Great selection of authentic local food plus international cuisine. Advance booking recommended. **€€€**

Sykaminia Eleftherias 26, old quarter; www.sikaminia.com. A much-loved *maeirkó* with archival photos of old Limassol adorning the walls. The menu stresses a few meat stews, simple fish fries like *marída*, and *óspria* (legume dishes), for which every table has a few onions (the usual garnish) poised at the ready. Fresh *goutsiá* (broad beans) with greens and celery are very good indeed. Bulk wine is surprisingly pricey. **€-€€**

Syrian Restaurant Iliados 3, Potamos Germasogias tourist district; www.syrianrestaurantlimassol.com.cy. All the Syrian/Lebanese favourites are present and correct here: *mouhamara* (red pepper and walnut dip), *nakanek* sausages, *kibbeh* (bulgur wheat turnovers), *moutabhal* (aubergine dip). There's an à la carte menu, but two diners or more should opt for the famous *mezé* of 15 to 38 platters, according to party size. There are also three grades of *arak*, *zivanía*, *ouzo* and wine to drink. The best seats are in the lovely garden fronted by a kitsch rendition of the Palmyra ruins (your clue that you've found the place); the interior is rather dull, though there are *shishas* on offer, toked on by single Arab males, and loud music at weekends. **€€-€€€**

Troödos Mountains

Mylos Mylou 8, Old Kakopetria; www.millhotelcyprus.com. The *Mill Hotel*'s inviting restaurant, *Mylos,* has a menu filled with both authentic, traditional Cypriot fare and international dishes. Trout is one of the favourites here. It's best to book in advance because the place is popular and often busy. Ask for a table outside to take in the pretty village views from the balcony. **€€€**

Troodos Hotel Restaurant Troödos Square, Troödos; www.troodoshotel.com. This no-frills restaurant on Troödos Square serves up grilled fish and meat, pasta dishes and pizza. The food is quite good and affordable. Barbecue on Sundays. The spacious restaurant spills out onto a lovely outdoor terrace with panoramic mountain views. **€€**

Pafos and around

Finikas Central Square, Polis Chrysochous; www.finikasrestaurant.net. Housed in a fine old building right on the central square, *Finikas* has the air of being a cut above the usual tourist joint. It does a complete range of meals – fish, meat, charcoal grills, steak, Cypriot dishes, pasta, salads – and has kids' and vegetarian menus. House specials include a feta crusted chicken fillet, and duck with chili peppers and parsnip puree. **€€€**

Laona Votsi 6, Ktima (Upper Pafos); www.laonarestaurant.blogspot.com. This classic, very friendly marketplace *maeirkó*, inside a 1900-vintage interior (plus outdoors in summer), purveys such favourites as bean dishes, baked fish, rabbit stew, *kolokássia* with pork, as well as desserts like *palouzé* and *kaloprúma* (yoghurt, semolina and citrus-zest pie). The quaffable bulk wine is from Statós village. **€-€€**

Myrra Neapoleos 37, Ktima (Upper Pafos); www.myrratavern.com. This friendly family-run taverna offers good-value grills, mezé and wine. In summer, dishes incorporate fresh vegetables from the owners' garden. Reservations advisable, especially on Fridays and Saturdays when the place fills up quickly. **€€**

Sardegna di Gino Apostolou Pavlou 70, Shops 5–7, Kato Pafos; 26 933399. You're about to scoff the island's best wood-fired pizzas, courtesy of Sardinians Gino and Lisa. Be warned, 'small' means medium by most standards, 'medium' means large. There are giant salads, a short dessert list and Italian bulk or bottled wine. Eat indoors or out – or wherever there's space (booking advised). **€€**

7 St Georges Anthypolohagou Georgiou M Savva 37, west edge of Geroskipou; www.7stgeorges.com. George Demetriades, now assisted by his sons Ben and Damian, offers what could well be the widest ranging *mezé* on the island. All the ingredients are either organically grown or gathered wild by George; seasonally variable platters might include flash-fried *agrélia* (wild asparagus), goat-and-cumin *tavás*, sautéed wild *pángalos* greens, *tsamarélla* (goat), fried or pickled mushrooms and *kléftigo*. The quality of the food, the service and the old-taverna atmosphere are a world away from the anonymous *kalamári*-and-chips joints of Kato Pafos. Wine, dessert and coffee are charged separately, bumping it into the higher price category. **€€€**

Ta Perix Kioubilay 20, Moutallou district, Ktima (Upper Pafos); 99 628701. The town's best *mezé* house, where you tick off choices from a proffered order form: quail eggs, *agrélia*, *tyrokafterí* (Greek spicy cheese dip), grilled quail, chicken livers, boiled greens, mushrooms. You can even specify the size of platter (small or large). It's justifiably popular, with a small interior, so weekend reservations are mandatory. **€€**

Northern Cyprus

Northern Nicosia (Lefkoşa)

Ottoman Kebab House Bendrettin Demirel Street; www.merithotels.com. This low-key restaurant at the *Merit Hotel* (complete with a casino) serves authentic southeastern *mezé* and kebab, often to a soundtrack of traditional music. Book in advance. **€€€**

Rustem Kitabevi Girne Street; https://www.facebook.com/rustemkitabevi. Technically, this is a bookstore and a stunning one at that. In operation since 1937, it has a unique old-world charm. Aside from its selection of rare and common books (mainly in Turkish but also some in English), if you climb the wooden staircase, you'll come across a small restaurant serving homemade Cypriot food during the day. There's no menu, just a choice of the dishes of the day. A visit is well worthwhile, dining or not. **€€**

Sabor Latino Selimiye Meydanı 29; (392) 228 8322. This sleek coffee bar/bistro is somewhat misnamed now that the menu includes various Asian specials like spicy prawn soup, noodles with spinach and mushrooms and beef-vegetable stir-fry, all in hefty portions, alongside tapas and Italian platters. There's a full list of decadent western desserts, alcoholic drinks despite the mosque opposite, and excellent wait staff. Seating indoors or out, the latter with eyefuls of the Selimiye. **€€**

Sedirhan Büyük Han; (392) 2287760. Good selection of traditional Turkish snacks and meals served in the beautifully restored Büyük Han. Don't be put off by the picture menu – it's actually very useful if you don't know the cuisine. Even if you're not hungry, stop for a drink – it's such a marvellous setting. **€€€**

Keryneia (Girne) and around

Canli Balik Eski Liman; (392) 815 11 23. This is a good fish restaurant down by the harbour (roughly halfway around, below the Folk Art Museum) and cheaper than many. The menu includes a wide selection of non-seafood main courses as well, including lamb shank, sea bass and sea bream, kebabs, kléftiko, omelettes, egg and chips and burgers, together with set menus. Opt for the fish. **€€€**

Lagoon Kordonboyu 11; (392) 815 6555. The best seafood tavern in town for some years now, and the upper-deck, bay-view tables with proper table linen are unbeatable. Choose between seafood mezé – a modest dozen platters – or wild-caught fish by the kilo, accompanied by rocket salad and grilled *hellim*. Drinks are from the St Hilarion microwinery. **€€€**

Famagusta (Gazİmağusa)

Aspava 19 Liman Yolu Street; www.facebook.com/aspavamagusa.The Aspava looks out onto the main town square and mosque and offers not only grills and mezé, with food served in a shady garden, but is a prime people-watching site. **€€€**

Historia Namik Kemal Meydani; (392) 862 1199. Set on the main square of Famagusta, this unassuming little spot is an ideal spot for people-watching over a bite to eat. Expect a variety of grilled meat dishes and kebab, along with less inspiring options like omelettes, burgers and chicken. The History Special – lamb marinated in garlic and yoghurt – is well worth a try. **€€**

Petek 1 Yesil Deniz Street (where it intersects with Liman Yolu Street, opposite the Sea Gate); www.petekpastahanesi.com. Part of a chain of patisseries (or *pastahanesi*), *Petek* offers a wide range of sweets, Turkish Delight, ice cream and various types of cake, most involving combinations of honey, chocolate and nuts. Housed in an odd-shaped building with terrace, balcony and potted plants, an attractively cluttered interior and a tempting cake counter beyond. **€**

Karpasia (Karpaz)

Hemingway's Restobar Karpaz Gate Marina, Aigaialousa (Yenierenköy); www.karpazbay.com. A vast, contemporary restaurant dishing up both international and traditional Cypriot cuisine. Pick from a wide selection of fish and meat dishes, washed down with a glass of wine from the extensive list. **€€€**

Oasis at Ayfilon Mersin 10, Rizokarpaso (Dipkarpaz); www.oasishotelkarpas.com. This laid-back spot at the *Ayfilon* hotel specializes in grilled dishes – lamb, chicken and fresh fish are always on the menu. Ask for a table on the sea-view terrace to catch the stunning sunset. **€€**

Travel essentials

Practical information

Accessibility

Cyprus is not widely known for being disability-friendly, unfortunately. Pavements are often in poor condition, blocked by parked cars or tree roots, and zebra crossings and wide paths are limited, though municipalities are working to improve the infrastructure.

Larnaka, Pafos, and Ercan airports have accessible restrooms, ramps, and charging stations for electric wheelchairs and staff are quick to assist if needed.

Buses with ramps and private taxis are the most accessible transport options – check Cyprus Accessible Transport (www.cyprusaccessible transport.com). Over forty beaches, including Coral Bay, Fig Tree Beach, Foinikoudes, McKenzie, and Dasoudi, have ramps for sea access. This is less common in northern Cyprus.

Restaurants and buildings are required to have wheelchair ramps and ground-floor disabled toilets. New establishments must meet these standards, though older ones may not.

Useful sites are: www.eudisabilitycard.gov.cy and www.opak.org.cy (Cyprus Paraplegic Organisation). The Ministry of Tourism has an excellent online guide Accessible Cyprus on its website www.visitcyprus.com

Accommodation

Heavily dependent on tourism, Cyprus offers a wide range of accommodation to suit every traveller.

Luxurious 5-star resorts with spas, sprawling gardens and generous breakfast buffets are easy to find – some ranked among Europe's best (anassa.com). For more alternative stays, eco-glamping sites and Mongolian-style yurts in quiet valleys offer unique experiences (aphroditecamping.com, yurtsincyprus.com).

For high season (mid-June to October) stays, booking in advance is essential. The Deputy Ministry of Tourism's (see page 140) 'Guide to Hotels and Other Tourist Establishments' lists licensed options and is available online at visitcyprus.com under the 'Accommodation' tab. Many are also on Booking.com and Airbnb, including licensed B&Bs and guesthouses.

In the north, https://hotelsofnorthcyprus.com provides listings. Northern hotels can be more affordable, though many cater to the casino scene. Most are in or around Keryneia, with modest but good options also found on the Karpasia Peninsula.

I'd like a single/double room **Tha íthela éna monóklino/ díklino**
What's the rate per night? **Póso stihízei giá mía nýkhta?**

Cyprus' range of hotels will please every type of traveller; solo, couples or families. Choose between five-star luxury havens and comfortable guesthouses to pleasant hotel-apartments in three grades. All-inclusive resorts, especially around Pafos, are beginning to multiply. All hotels offer discounts during low season, which for seaside resorts is from November to March, and for hill resorts from October to April – both excluding the Christmas/New Year and Easter weeks. Many beach hotels close from New Year to the end of March.

Self-catering villas are most numerous around Pafos, Ayia Napa and Keryneia, with lesser numbers in the Limassol foothills and around Larnaka. They are best rented through our recommended agencies (see below) or directly on Booking.com and Airbnb.

Through a Ministry of Tourism initiative, agrotourism has gained popularity amongst locals and visitors alike. Many traditional houses in the countryside have been renovated and are now rented out as holiday homes. For details, secure a copy of the booklet *Rural Cyprus: A Guide to Traditional Accommodation*, or access www.visitcyprus.com or www.agrotourism.com.cy, which also has a booking facility.

Securing a package deal through travel operators is still a popular and hassle-free option for many travellers. For the South, Sunvil (www.sunvil.co.uk) has a good selection of villas and agrotourist facilities, plus selected hotels; Top Kinisis (www.topkinisis.com) is one of the most renowned local travel agencies that's been running for three decades. For the North,

Cyprus Paradise (www.cyprusparadise.com) are specialists, with a wide range of resort hotels.

Airports

Larnaka International Airport (LCA; www.hermesairports.com), Cyprus' principal air gateway, lies 5km from Larnaka town and 50km from Nicosia. Dedicated airport shuttles run frequently between the airport and Pafos, Limassol (www.limassolairportexpress.eu) and Nicosia (www.kapnos airportshuttle.com). Only expensive private transfers are available for Agia Napa and Protaras. Several urban buses operate daily to Larnaka. A daytime taxi fare is about €15.

Pafos International Airport (PFO; www.hermesairports.com), 11km southeast of Pafos on the west coast, handles several no-frills airlines and many charter services. Local buses run frequently between the airport and Pafos. Daytime taxi fares range from €30 to the centre of Pafos up to €60 to Limassol, for which www.limassolairportexpress.eu is a better option.

Ercan International Airport (ECN; www.ercanhavalimani.aero) in Northern Cyprus, 14km east of Nicosia, is served by UK-originating flights which must stop in Turkey en route. There is a limited shuttle-bus service to Keryneia, north Nicosia and Famagusta. Taxis serve all points in the North, expensively.

Apps

Several free apps can make your stay in Cyprus smoother. For transport, Bolt operates in all major southern cities and now includes an option to request a female driver for added safety. For navigation, Google Maps and Waze are popular – Waze also alerts users to cameras, speed limits, and police. The Cyprus Bus app provides up-to-date routes and schedules. For eco-friendly travel, Next Bike offers on-demand bike rentals in Pafos, Larnaka, Limassol, Nicosia, and Famagusta. Craving food or drinks? Foody and Wolt deliver everything from fast food and groceries to specialty coffee and cocktails.

Bicycle and motorcycle hire

You can hire bikes and motorcycles in all important southern resorts, though motorbike hire is overpriced and thus not popular, especially given local car-driver habits. You must be at least 18 years of age and hold the correct licence; 17-year-olds may hire a moped of maximum 49cc. Crash helmets must be worn by both driver and pillion passengers; reputable agencies supply them.

Mountain biking, particularly in the Troödos or Pentadaktylos (Beşparmak) mountains, and on the Akamas Peninsula, is popular but strenuous. Cycling along coastal back roads is far easier. The Ministry of Tourism (see page 140) contains extensive information on cycling in Cyprus (www.visitcyprus.com), detailing many routes. For more details, contact the Cyprus Cycling Federation; www.cypruscycling.org .

Budgeting for your trip

Pricewise, Cyprus is above average as a Mediterranean destination – more expensive than most Greek islands, Turkey, much of Spain and southern Portugal, about the same as provincial France, but cheaper than Italy. In high season, airfares from Britain cost around £300–400 and a good four-star hotel room will be about €150–200 per night. For the North, airfares are about the same, though lodging costs somewhat less. Booking a package, particularly at the last minute, will save you money; see our agency recommendations above.

Food and drink prices across the island have increased (a three-course meal without drinks in a simple restaurant usually costs about €25–35 per person). Drinks in bars and restaurants range from €3.50 for a beer in a simple place to €10 and over for cocktails in a fancy establishment. Wine is relatively expensive in the North. Museum entry is generally inexpensive, ranging from under a euro to €5.

The Cypriot Department of Antiquities offers 1-, 3- and 7-day special entry cards (€8.50, €17 and €25, respectively), valid in all museums and monuments which are part of the Department of Antiquities, including Pafos, Larnaka, Limassol and Kolossi castles and the Hala Sultan Tekke. The cards are available at the ticket offices of each participating museum/monument; www.mcw.gov.cy/mcw/da/da.nsf/DMLmuseums_en.

Car hire

As many sights in Cyprus are spread out, and beyond the reach of public transport, it is worth hiring a car. To hire a car in the South, you must have a valid national driver's licence (held for at least three years) or, for non-EU nationals, an International Driving Permit. Depending on the company, the minimum age is 21 to 25. A deposit is usually required, payable by credit card. Check whether driving on unsurfaced roads will invalidate the insurance.

The most effective way of booking a car in advance is via a consolidator website like www.comparecarrentals.co.uk, www.auto-europe.co.uk, or www.skyscanner.net/carhire. Popular car rental agencies in the south include Avis (avis.com), EuropCar (Europcar.com) and Herz (hertz.com). Rates, always with unlimited mileage, begin as low as €10 per day for the smallest compact in winter, more than doubling in summer. For a decent family-sized car, plan on spending at least €35 per day in high season. If you do not have an annual CDW insurance policy (these are well worth it if you hire cars more than two weeks annually; try www.insurance4carhire.com), you'll need to add another few euros per day. In summer, air conditioning is strongly recommended.

If you rent a car in the south, many companies will not allow you to cross to the north – check when arranging the rental. Where companies do allow you to cross into the north, most will not arrange insurance – you'll need to arrange your own at the crossing point – there will be a booth where you can do this.

I'd like to hire a car (tomorrow) for one day/a week
Tha íthela na nikiáso éna aftokínito (ávrio) giá mía méra/ mía evdomáda
(international) driving licence **(diethnís) díploma**

Climate

Cyprus enjoys sunny skies and low humidity, except for in the summer.

On the coast, sea breezes temper the 32°C (90°F) heat of July and August, but in Nicosia you can add 3–4 degrees on average, and the thermometer inland often goes above 37°C (99°F).

January through March see snowfalls in the Troödos mountain range – most seasons there is enough to permit skiing. The last few years have seen heavy rain between November and March, but there are plenty of fine days too, and the sea temperature remains just warm enough for swimming until New Year. Spring can be particularly dusty with winds blowing in from Africa.

The following are average coastal temperatures:

	J	F	M	A	M	J	J	A	S	O	N	D
max												
ºC	17	19	21	23	27	31	32	31	27	23	18	17
ºF	63	63	69	73	80	87	90	87	80	80	64	64
min												
ºC	6	7	9	12	16	19	21	21	20	16	12	9
ºF	42	44	48	54	61	66	70	70	68	61	54	48

Crime and safety

Despite a spike in crime rates, Cyprus is a relatively safe country. The biggest crime scandals are by organised groups and political corruption that are unlikely to affect a traveller. Still, you might witness violence in drunken brawls and a few scams at tourist hotspots. Burglaries and car thefts are on the rise, however. Otherwise, take the same precautions as you would at home.

A brush with the law rather than criminals is a far more likely scenario during a visit to the island. Speed limits are strictly enforced, and driving with above the (low) permitted levels of alcohol in the blood or breath carries severe penalties. Road cameras along avenues of the big cities and along highways have been enforced leading to a spike in fines, so drive carefully.

Driving

Road conditions. Driving conditions are generally good in Cyprus, with well-surfaced, well-marked 'B' roads and fast motorways ('A') running along the south coast, linking Limassol, Larnaka, Agia Napa and Pafos, and heading inland to Nicosia. Beware of speeding, as there are regular radar-gun traps.

Are we on the right road for ...? **Páme kalá giá ...?**
left/right **aristerá/dexiá**
Full tank, please. **Óso pérnei, parakaló**
super/normal/diesel **soúper/aplí/dízel**
My car has broken down. **To amáxi mou éhei páthi vlávi.**
There's been an accident. **Égine éna atýhima.**

Main roads are paved and in good condition, and even many of the tertiary ('E') roads are easily negotiated. Short distances on minor ('F') roads, typically in the hills, can often be tackled in an ordinary car, but they are narrow (one-lane) and often unpaved, in addition to having steep, hairpin turns. A four-wheel-drive vehicle is best for the many rough tracks.

With the exception of the main roads between Nicosia and Keryneia, Morfou and Famagusta, the main coastal road east of Keryneia, and the main trunk road up the Karpasia Peninsula, roads in the North are often in poor condition.

In the cities, traffic is fairly orderly. During the rush hour, expect traffic jams in Nicosia, Keryneia, Larnaka, Limassol and Pafos, especially leaving town in the early evening.

Rules and regulations. British and Irish motorists will feel at home in Cyprus, where traffic keeps to the left and roundabouts are frequent. Seat-belt use is compulsory in the front of cars and, where fitted, in the back, too. Drunk-driving control points are frequent at weekends and penalties stiff. Always carry your driving licence and car-hire documents with you.

Speed limits. The usual speed limits are 50kmh (30mph) in town and

100kmh (60mph) on motorways (lower limits may be posted).

Fuel. The price of petrol in Cyprus compares well with elsewhere in Europe – certainly less than in Greece, Italy, France or Britain. Diesel is cheaper, and it is possible to hire diesel cars. Filling stations generally close on Sundays and public holidays, but all have self-service fuel pumps that take cash or credit cards. They are plentiful in and around the main towns and resorts, but are rare in the mountains. If you're setting out on a back-country excursion, make sure the tank is full.

Parking. This is often difficult in Nicosia, Keryneia, Limassol, Pafos, Agia Napa and Larnaka. Fines are given for illegal parking. Try to find a meter or car park, or be willing to park in an uncontrolled residential area and walk a bit.

Problems. Call your hire company first. In an emergency, call the police (see emergency numbers, below).

Road signs. Most road signs, and most other signs imparting general information, use the standard international pictographs, and all written signs appear twice: once in Greek, once in English. In the North, signs are in Turkish and English.

Electricity

The standard current is 240 volts, 50 Hz ac; sockets are usually three-pin, as in the UK. Most hotels and some villas have 110-volt outlets for razors. Plug adaptors (*adaptores prizas*), if necessary, may be provided free by hotels, or are available in bigger supermarkets and electrical merchants.

Embassies and consulates

The following embassies and consulates are all in Southern Nicosia:

Australia: High Commission, Pindarou 27, Block A, Level 7; 22 753001, www.cyprus.embassy.gov.au

Canada: Honorary Consulate, Margarita House 402, Themistokli Dervi 15; 22 775508

Ireland: Embassy, Aiantos 7; 22 818183, www.dfa.ie/irish-embassy/cyprus

UK: High Commission, Alexandrou Pallis; 22 861100, www.gov.uk/world/

organisations/british-high-commission-nicosia
US: Embassy, Corner Metochiou and Ploutarchou, Egkomi; 22 393939, https://cy.usembassy.gov

Emergencies

Republic of Cyprus

Police, ambulance and fire brigade: **112**
Forest fires: **1407**

Northern Cyprus

Police: **155**
Ambulance: **112**
Fire brigade**: 199**
Forest fires **177**

Getting there

For most people, air travel is the only practical way of getting to Cyprus. Direct scheduled and charter flights link numerous British airports to Larnaka and Pafos. The flying time is around 4 hours 30 minutes. In addition to the many chartered airlines that fly to Cyprus, carriers with scheduled services from the UK include **British Airways** (www.britishairways.com), **easyJet** (www.easyjet.com), **Jet 2** (www.jet2.com), **Ryanair** (www.ryanair.com) and **WizzAir** (www.wizzair.com).

Turkish airlines fly to Northern Cyprus from abroad via an intermediate stop in Turkey. Best of the carriers with service from England is **Pegasus** (www.flypgs.com) or **AJet** (www.ajet.com).

Health and medical care

Medical treatment and assistance is offered free of charge to tourists in case of emergency, but it is recommended that you take out travel insurance to cover illness and accident while on holiday. Visitors from Ireland and other EU countries should bring along a European Health Insurance card (EHIC), which allows for free casualty ward medical treatment. UK nationals can continue to use their EHIC up until the card's expiry date, and then they should obtain a Global Health Insurance Card (GHIC) card (www.nhs.uk/using-the-nhs/healthcare-abroad).

There are very capable doctors and dentists in the resorts, cities and larger towns, as well as good hospital facilities. Your hotel will advise you of the nearest English-speaking doctor. After-hours doctors are listed in local newspapers or can be contacted as follows: Nicosia, 90 901432; Agia Napa, 90 901433; Larnaka, 90 901414; Limassol, 90 901415; Pafos, 90 901416.

Stomach upsets should not be a problem, as hotels and restaurants observe high standards of cleanliness. Tap water is safe but often unpalatable; springs in the Troödos are much better. Be sure to apply plenty of suncream and try to avoid the scorching heat of the day.

A **pharmacy** *(farmakío)* is recognized by the sign outside – a green cross on a white background. They are generally open Monday–Friday 8am–1pm and 3 or 4–7pm (mornings only on Wednesday and Saturday). Certain pharmacies offer a 24-hour service – daily updates are available on ygeia-news.com/dianyktereyonta-farmakeia

Most medicines sold in the UK, US, Canada and Europe are available, but may require a prescription. Pharmacists can generally advise on minor ailments.

Where's the nearest (all-night) pharmacy? **Pou íne to kondinótero farmakío pou efimerévei?**
I need a doctor/dentist **Hriázome éna giatró/odontogiatró**
an ambulance **éna asthenofóro**
the hospital **to nosokomío**

Language

English is spoken almost as a second language in all the resorts, and is understood by many people in Cyprus, both North and South. It is only well off the beaten track that a familiarity with Greek (in Southern Cyprus)

or Turkish (in Northern Cyprus) is useful. If you do speak Greek or Turkish, be aware that the country dialects of each language spoken on Cyprus will be difficult to follow when you get a reply but it will still be useful to communicate.

Α	α	a	as in 'bar'
Β	β	v	as in 'veto'
Γ	γ	g	as in 'go' (before i- and e-sounds, pronounced like y in 'yes')
Δ	δ	d	like th in 'this'
Ε	ε	e	as in 'get'
Ζ	ζ	z	same as in English
Η	η	i	as in 'ski'
Θ	θ	th	as in 'thin'
Ι	ι	i	as in 'ski'
Κ	κ	k	same as in English
Λ	λ	l	same as in English
Μ	μ	m	same as in English
Ν	ν	n	same as in English
Ξ	ξ	x	as in 'box'
Ο	ο	o	as in 'road'
Π	π	p	in Cypriot, pronounced as hard 'b'
Ρ	ρ	r	same as in English
Σ	σ	s	as in 'kiss'
Τ	τ	t	same as in English
Υ	υ	y	as in 'country'
Φ	φ	f	same as in English
Χ	χ	ch, h	as in Scottish 'loch'
Ψ	ψ	ps	as in tipsy
Ο/Ω	ω	o	as in 'road'
ΑΙ	αι	e	as in hay

ΑΥ	αυ	av	as in avant-garde
ΕΙ	ει	i	as in ski
ΕΥ	ευ	ev	as in ever
ΟΙ	οι	i	as in ski
ΟΥ	ου	ou	as in soup
ΓΓ	γγ	ng	as in longer
ΓΚ	γκ	g	as in gone
ΓΞ	γξ	nx	as in anxious
ΜΠ	μπ	b or mb	as in beg or compass
ΝΤ	ντ	d or nd	as in dog or under

The table above lists the Greek alphabet with their capital and small forms, followed by the letter(s) to which they correspond in English. Below are a few phrases you might want to use:

hello **yásoo (informal), yásas (formal)**
good morning **kaliméra**
good afternoon/evening **kalispéra**
good night **kaliníkhta**
please **parakaló**
thank you **evharistó**
yes **ne**
no **óhi**
I don't speak Greek. **Den miló elliniká.**
I don't understand. **Den katalavéno.**
What does this mean? **Ti siméni aftó?**
Do you speak English? **Miláte angliká?**
excuse me **me sinhoríte**
where/when/how **pou/póte/pos**
yesterday/today/tomorrow **khthes/símera/ávrio**
big/small **megálo/mikró**

cheap/expensive **ftinó/akrivó**
open/closed **aniktó/klistó**
here/there **dó/ekí**
early/late **norís/argá**
How much is that? **Póso kánei aftó?**

LGBTQ+ travellers

Southern Cyprus has a small but growing LGBTQ+ scene, and slowly improving acceptance of both the local LGBTQ+ community and visitors from off-island. More traditional Cypriots can display prejudiced attitudes to **gay people** and overt public behaviour might attract disapproving frowns and the clicking of tongues. However, gay clubs and events do exist in large towns and Pride celebrations happen annually organised by ACCEPT-LGBTI Cyprus (accept.cy) that's active in social, cultural and political circles. Northern Cyprus is considerably more conservative, but there is a growing number of active groups like the Queer Cyprus Association (www.queercyprus.org).

Media

Newspapers and magazines. There is a good selection of British and Irish newspapers and major American weekly news magazines available, sometimes a day after publication. The *Cyprus Mail*, Cyprus' leading English-language daily (not Mon; www.cyprus-mail.com), has current news coverage and a good What's On section. *Cyprus Today* is a weekly English language circulation that covers the North and South in addition to international news, entertainment and sports (www.cyprustodayonline.com).

Radio and TV. The Cyprus Broadcasting Corporation (CyBC; www.cybc.com.cy) transmits English-language programmes from 6pm until midnight on its Second Programme. Radio BFBS (British Forces Broadcasting Service; www.bfbs.com) is on the air 24 hours a day, at various frequencies. Some hotels have BBC Radio Five Live. Multi-star hotels offer cable and satellite television channels, including BBC World News, CNN and Sky. British sporting events can be watched on television in bars that subscribe to Sky Sports and/or the BBC.

Money

Currency. The euro is the national currency of Southern Cyprus. Cypriot euro coins have images of the indigenous moufflon sheep (1, 2 and 5 cents), the ancient Kyrenia ship (10, 20 and 50 cents), and the prehistoric idol of Pomos (€1 and €2). The euro banknotes are €5, €10, €20, €50, €100, €200 and €500.

In Northern Cyprus, the Turkish lira (TL) is the local currency. However, euros, pounds and dollars are accepted in hotels, restaurants and other businesses, albeit sometimes at a discount.

Banking. All banks, both South and North, are equipped with ATMs accepting foreign cards. Travellers' cheques are rarely accepted, or with great suspicion and delay, so are not worth the trouble. In the North, the best way to change euro or sterling into TL is at the numerous exchange (*döviz*) bureaux in Nicosia and Keryneia.

Credit cards. Major credit cards are welcome as payment by all car-hire firms, in most hotels, restaurants or shops.

I want to change some pounds/dollars. **Thélo na alláxo merikés líres sterlínes/meriká dollária.**

Can I pay with this credit card? **Boró na pliróso me aftí ti pistotikí kárta?**

Opening hours

National museums and archaeological sites. These vary considerably, though always with very short hours on Sunday, if open at all. **Banks.** Monday–Friday 8m–2pm, sometimes until 2pm on Friday depending on the branch.

Shops. Southern shops are generally open Mon–Sat 8am–8pm (closing half an hour later mid-summer). Shops in the malls do not close during lunch and most have longer hours over Christmas. There are no afternoon hours on Wednesday and Sunday year-round. Northern schedules are similar: notionally in summer Monday–Saturday 8am–1.30pm, and Monday–Friday 2.30–6.30pm (not Wednesday); big supermarkets may open Sundays. In winter, expect opening Monday–Saturday 8am–6pm.

Are you open tomorrow? **Íste aniktó ávrio?**

Police

The national police headquarters are off the Limassol-bound road in southeastern Nicosia, and there are divisional offices and stations in all main towns and resorts. Regular police officers in southern Cyprus wear blue uniforms and cruise around in blue-and-white police cars. Most members of the police (**Astynomía** in Greek; **Polis** in Turkish) speak some English. You'll recognize traffic policemen (common in Nicosia rush hours) by their white-and-blue uniform.

Where's the nearest police station? **Pou íne to kondinótero astynomikó tmíma?**

Public holidays

In addition to their own national holidays, Cypriots also celebrate certain Greek or Turkish holidays. Offices close on the following days. Shops remain open on some holidays: ask locally which ones. 'S' means in the South, 'N' means in the North.

1 Jan *Protohroniá* New Year's Day (S, N)

6 Jan *Theofánia* Epiphany (S)

25 Mar *Ikostipémptis Martíou (tou Evangelismoú)* Greek Independence Day (S)

1 Apr *Iméra Enárxeos Kypriakoú* Greek Cypriot National Day (S)

23 Apr National Sovereignty Day (N)

1 May *Protomagiá* Labour Day (S, N)
19 May Youth & Sport Day (N)
20 Jul Peace Operation Day (N)
1 Aug TMT Day (N)
15 Aug *Dekapendávgoustos (tis Panagías)* Dormition of the Virgin (S)
30 Aug Victory Day (N)
1 Oct *Iméra tis Anexartisías (tis Kýprou)* Cyprus Independence Day (S)
28 Oct *Ikostiogdóis Oktovríou ('Ohi')* 'No' Day, commemorating Greek defiance of Italian invasion of 1940 (S)
29 Oct Turkish Republic Day (N)
15 Nov TRNC Day (N)
25 Dec *Hristoúgenna* Christmas Day (S)
26 Dec *Sýnaxi tis Panagías* Gathering of the Virgin (S)

Movable dates

Katharí Deftéra 1st Day of Lent/ (also known as Green or Clean Monday) (S)
Megáli Paraskeví Good Friday (S)
Deftéra tou Páskha Easter Monday (S)
Kataklysmós Pentecost (Festival of the Flood) (S)
Şeker Bayramı (N)
Mevlûd (N)
Kurban Bayramı (N)

Religion

You should dress modestly when visiting churches, monasteries and mosques. The dress code for monasteries is usually rigidly enforced and specifies long trousers for men, a below-the-knee skirt/dress for women and covered shoulders for both sexes. Churches are generally less formal. You must remove your shoes before entering a mosque.

Telephone

To call Southern Cyprus from abroad, the international dialling code is 357; for the North it is 90. Area codes do not exist in southern Cyprus, merely eight-digit subscriber numbers. In Nicosia, they start with 22; Agia Napa 23; Larnaka 24; Limassol 25; Pafos 26. All mobiles begin with 9. The fixed-line area code for the entire North, which you use after 90, is 392; mobile codes are 533, 535, and 542. Northern subscriber numbers consist of seven digits; for land lines, omit 392 within the country, but you must use the codes when dialling mobiles. To make international calls from Cyprus, dial 00, then the country code.

It may be worth getting a pay-as-you-go SIM upon arrival. The three companies are CYTA-Vodaphone, EPIC and Primetel; CYTA-Vodaphone SIMs come with some talk time and are valid for 3 months – top it up once, and the number remains valid for a year. In the North, you'd do very well to get a local pay-as-you-go plan on local companies Türkcell or Telsim, as roaming with your home SIM can result in some shocking bills.

Time zones

The chart below shows the time differences between Cyprus, which is on Eastern European Time (EET), and various cities in winter (UTC/GMT + 2 hours). In summer, clocks advance 1 hour, so the time difference with the UK and US stays the same.

New York	London	**Cyprus**	Jo'burg	Sydney	Auckland
5am	10am	**noon**	noon	9pm	11pm

Tipping

Service charges are included in hotel and restaurant bills, but a little extra is always appreciated, especially for good service, to porters and chambermaids. Taxi drivers, hair stylists, servers and tour guides all expect tips.

Toilets

In the South, a few public toilets exist in parks of larger towns but are not well kept. Museums often have the cleanest facilities. In the North, pay toilets are conspicuous around old Nicosia, Keryneia harbour and Famagusta, but you'll prefer to use restaurant or hotel loos. They are indicated with the usual pictographs.

Where are the toilets? **Pou íne ta apohoritíria?**

Tourist information

The **Deputy Ministry of Tourism or its sub-brand Visit Cyprus**; www.visitcyprus.com), which covers the **South**, is a mine of information, with free brochures and maps.

UK: 13 St James's Square, London, SW1Y 4LB; (020) 7321 4170

In Cyprus, the tourist offices maintains offices at **Larnaka Airport** arrivals, at **Pafos Airport** arrivals, at **Limassol old port square**, and in the following major tourist centres: Nicosia old town (marked on our map), Limassol centre (marked on map), Larnaka, Pafos (marked on map), Agia Napa, Polis, Pano Platres, and Paralimni.

For information on **Northern Cyprus:**

UK: 29 Bedford Square, London, WC1B 3ED; (020) 7631 1930; www.welcometonorthcyprus.co.uk.

US: 1667 K Street, Suite 690, Washington DC, 20006; (202) 887 6198

In Northern Cyprus, there are tourist offices in **Keryneia/Girne** on the old port, **Famagusta/Gazimağusa** old town by the Land Gate, and **Nicosia/Lefkoşa** in the Keryneia/Girne Gate.

Transport

Cyprus has no railways and the inter-urban bus service is not always frequent, especially on Sundays or to/from remote villages – just one or two departures per day, if that. Bus services within the towns and resorts, however, are good. Private and shared taxis fill the public transport gap.

Private taxis. Vehicles are metered. You can hail a taxi on the street or call for one by telephone.

Shared service taxis. In the South, service taxis (actually minibuses) take from four to eight passengers and connect all major towns every half-hour.

The main nationwide company is Travel & Express, fares and booking on 7777 7474 or www.travelexpress.com.cy. Prices are fixed and quite reasonable. In the North, minibuses called *dolmuş* operate between the towns but only depart when they are full.

Where can I get a taxi/service taxi/minibus? **Pou boró na vro éna taxí/yperastiká taxi?**

Visas and entry requirements

Entering the Republic. Nationals of the EU, the UK, Australia, Canada, Japan, New Zealand, Singapore, the US and some other countries can stay in Cyprus for up to three months without a visa. Legal points of entry are the ports of Larnaka, Limassol and Pafos, and the international airports of Larnaka and Pafos.

Entering the North. Visitors travelling via Ercan Airport or the ports of Famagusta (Gazimağusa) or Keryneia (Girne) can explore the Turkish-controlled Northern Cyprus but will have issues if they want to cross to the south. The republic's position is still that anybody entering the north through the illegal ports or airports, might face legal sanctions and crossing to the south will be complicated as they will be considered to have entered the country through unofficial points of arrival – even if no entry stamp for the North is actually recorded in their passport.

Index

MINI
CYPRUS

Second Edition 2025

Editor: Kate Drynan
Author: Eleni Philippou
Picture Manager: Tom Smyth
Cartography Update: Katie Bennett
Layout: Danielle Titmas
Production Operations Manager: Katie Bennett
Publishing Technology Manager: Rebeka Davies
Head of Publishing: Sarah Clark
Photography Credits: Caroline Jones/Apa Publications 52; Dreamstime 88; George Taylor/Apa Publications 12TL, 40; iStock 12CL, 12BR, 13CT, 13CB, 14T, 27, 36, 39, 57, 60, 65, 80; Jon Davidson/Apa Publications 45; Paul Murphy/Apa Publications 23; Shutterstock 1, 7, 8, 11, 12TR, 12BL, 12CR, 13T, 13B, 14CL, 14BR, 14BL, 16T, 16CL, 16BL, 16BR, 18T, 18CL, 18BL, 18BR,, 20, 24, 29, 30, 32, 35, 42, 46, 49, 51, 55, 59, 62, 67, 68, 70, 72, 74, 77, 78, 82, 85, 86, 90, 93, 94, 96, 99, 101, 103, 105, 106, 108, 110
Cover Credits: Pink church **Shutterstock**

About the author
Eleni Philippou is a travel writer based in her native Cyprus who is passionate about sharing the tales and treasures of her island. Her articles and features (published in *The Guardian*, *Culture Trip*, *Visit Nicosia* and more) highlight people's stories and encourage readers to engage with the local community. Art, culture and social community projects are her area of focus as the *Cyprus Mail's* What's On and Features writer. When she is not writing, she photographs events, performs in an Afro-Brazilian percussion band, and makes cyanotype art. Her website is www.eleniphilippou.com, although she is more active on Instagram @eleniphilippou28

Distribution
UK, Ireland and Europe: Apa Publications (UK) Ltd; mail@roughguides.com
United States and Canada: Two Rivers; ips@ingramcontent.com
Australia and New Zealand: Woodslane; info@woodslane.com.au
Worldwide: Apa Publications (UK) Ltd; mail@roughguides.com

Printed by Finidr in Czech Republic

ISBN: 9781835292549

Special Sales, Content Licensing and CoPublishing
Rough Guides can be purchased in bulk quantities at discounted prices. We can create special editions, personalized jackets and corporate imprints tailored to your needs.
mail@roughguides.com
roughguides.com

EU Representative
LOGOS EUROPE, 9 rue Nicolas Poussin, 17000, LA ROCHELLE, France; Contact@logoseurope.eu; +33 (0) 667937378

This book was produced using **Typefi** automated publishing software.

A catalogue record for this book is available from the British Library

Contact us
Every effort has been made to ensure that this publication is accurate, free from safety risks, and provides accurate information. However, changes and errors are inevitable. The publisher is not responsible for any resulting loss, inconvenience, injury or safety concerns arising from the use of this book. If you notice any errors, outdated information, or potential safety risks, please send your comments with the subject line "Rough Guide Mini Cyprus Update" to mail@roughguides.com.